PRAYER PUPS CHRISTIAN COMICS
FOUR PANELS

BY JEFFREY SMITH

ISBN 978-0-557-78098-3

First printing: November, 2010

"Where Did The Prayer Pups Come From?"

That's the second-most often asked question I get from fans of the Pups ("where do you come up with the ideas" is first, but more on that in a moment).

In 2007, I was working on a comic strip idea called "Stinky Shark." I had written hundreds of gags that I thought were pretty funny and I had designed a great shark character. Now all I needed was a group of supporting characters to round out the strip.

As I worked on the character design of Stinky's friends Leo, Abby and Star, I began to feel God pressing upon me to use the comic strip format to spread His Word. As I doodled crude characters searching for the right design, I also began reworking the gags to be not only funny, but to also be true to Christian principles.

I quickly recognized that Stinky Shark was the wrong venue for such an endeavor, and began thinking about what the strip should be instead. "Noah's Critters" jumped into my head and I dove into designing various animals to populate the strip.

Then two events happened that quickly prevented Noah's Critters from seeing the light of day. First, someone told me that "Noah's Critters" was a song by Peter, Paul and Mary. That could spell copyright problems. Secondly, I noticed that all of my animals looked like dogs. At that moment, Prayer Pups was born.

The star would be Con, the pug. My wife, Beany, and I had a precious little pug named Bubu and I wanted to highlight the pug character as not only the leader of the strip, but also as the character who provides the Biblical instruction.

But as I wrote the gags, drew the comics and showed them to friends, it became clear that Nim, the chihuahua was going to steal the show. His inappropriate statements and wild proclamations made him everyone's favorite character. And by showing how Christians should NOT to act, I was able to add a lot of humor while getting the message across.

I showed my primitive attempts to my Pastor, Dr. Kevin McCallon of Kingwood First Baptist Church and he suggested that I use the strips to create some children's church bulletins. He then connected me with the church's Children's Ministry team to help me develop a new kind of children's church bulletin.

Jonathan Brown, KFBC's former Children's Minister, and Sharon Wood, KFBC's Children's Associate, showed me the bulletins they were using and said the children were bored with them. I gathered their suggestions and Beany and I locked ourselves away writing and drawing. Within a few days, The Good Newz Children's Church Bulletins (www.thegoodnewz.org) were born.

I quickly added more churches across the country as I posted new comic strips everyday to the Prayer Pups website (www.prayerpups.com). The Pups' audience quickly grew in the U.S. and around the world. Soon, The Good Newz was being used in not only in U.S. churches, but in Canada, Japan, Europe and in many military chapels worldwide.

The Pups have been featured in magazines and newsletters and bulletins in more than two dozen countries, but the one place they've never seen the light of day is in a newspaper. After being rejected by every comic syndicate in the United States, I gave up on the traditional route of comic strip syndication and it hasn't seemed to make any difference in the success of the strip. In fact, with the challenges many newspapers are facing today, it might have been a blessing to be rejected.

People send me emails and messages telling me how much they enjoy the Pups and what they mean to the children in their churches. I read every note, and it's sometimes overwhelming that my little cartoons can touch people to such an extent that they take the time to write a message to thank me for the work I do.

But now it's my turn to thank you. I want to thank you for buying this book and for supporting something as off-the-wall as a comic strip ministry. I want to thank you for reading the Prayer Pups and for sharing them with your friends and family. I want to thank you for your generous encouragement over the years.

And I want to thank God for giving me the opportunity to minister by doing something I love.

I'm truly grateful.

Jeffrey Smith
Kingwood Texas
November, 2010

P.S., I get my ideas from the Bible, friends, family and everything else God has blessed me with.

WHAT I BELIEVE

- I believe the Bible is the eternal, infallible, authoritative Word of God.
- I believe there is only one God, forever existent in three entities: The Father, The Son, and The Holy Spirit.
- I believe in the absolute deity of Jesus Christ. I believe He was born of a virgin, walked a sinless life, died on the cross for our sins, was resurrected in the flesh, ascended to Heaven to be at the right hand of The Father, and in His future return.
- I believe people can receive forgiveness of sins and eternal life only through Jesus Christ.
- I believe the meaning of life is to pursue a closer relationship with God through the word of Jesus Christ.
- I believe it is wrong to portray Jesus or any other Biblical figure as a cartoon character, and you won't see it in Prayer Pups comics...ever!

MY MISSION

My aim in creating Prayer Pups comics is to help children and adults pursue a stronger relationship with Jesus Christ and to nurture a better understanding of The Word by using the gift with which God blessed me.

FOR BEANY, FOR BEING THERE EVERY TIME I NEED YOU, NO MATTER WHAT SILLY THING I'M ATTEMPTING

AND FOR BUBU, CASEY AND NEWTON, FOR BEING MY OWN LITTLE PRAYER PUPS

MEET THE PUPS

CONSTANTINE "CON"
A little pug with a lot of common sense. Con often helps the others find the truth of God's Word.

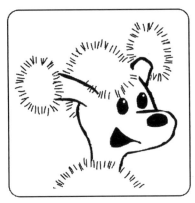

ABIGAIL "ABBY"
A poodle who loves looking pretty. God's always watching, so she wants to look her best.

NIMROD "NIM"
A chihuahua who usually speaks before he thinks, often resulting in ridiculous opinions.

AMOS
His desire for food is only outweighed by his love for God...but it's a really close call.

JEREMIAH "JERRY"
This dalmation thinks everyone should have spots. Jerry loves to tell really corny jokes.

PRAYER PUPS BY JEFFREY SMITH

IT'S A NEW YEAR AND A NEW OPPORTUNITY TO GROW AS A CHRISTIAN.

PRAYER PUPS BY JEFFREY SMITH

YOU CAN READ ABOUT JESUS AT THE TEMPLE AS A BOY IN LUKE 2:39-52.

PRAYER PUPS BY JEFFREY SMITH

MUSIC IS ONE OF THE MOST CREATIVE WAYS TO SPREAD THE WORD OF GOD.

PRAYER PUPS BY JEFFREY SMITH

THE STORY OF JESUS AND THE MONEYCHANGERS IS DETAILED IN ALL FOUR GOSPELS.

www.PrayerPups.com

PRAYER PUPS BY JEFFREY SMITH

IT'S NOT WHAT YOU WEAR THAT'S IMPORTANT, IT'S WHO YOU PUT YOUR FAITH IN!

www.PrayerPups.com

PRAYER PUPS BY JEFFREY SMITH

WE EACH ALREADY HAVE OUR OWN PERSONAL "HOTLINE TO HEAVEN." IT'S CALLED PRAYER.

www.PrayerPups.com

PRARER PUPS BY JEFFREY SMITH

THE BOOK OF JOB INSPIRED THE POPULAR SAYING "THE PATIENCE OF JOB."

www.PrayerPups.com

PRAYER PUPS BY JEFFREY SMITH

GOD CREATED YOU IN HIS IMAGE. THAT MEANS YOU'RE CREATIVE TOO!

www.PrayerPups.com

PRAYER PUPS BY JEFFREY SMITH

YOU CAN GET PRAYER PUPS COMICS IN YOUR EMAIL EVERYDAY! SIGN UP AT OUR WEBSITE.

www.PrayerPups.com

PRAYER PUPS BY JEFFREY SMITH

READ THE ENTIRE STORY OF JESUS AND THE SAMARITAN WOMAN IN JOHN 4:7-22   www.PrayerPups.com

PRAYER PUPS BY JEFFREY SMITH

WE ALL HAVE THE POWER TO INTERCEDE ON OTHER PEOPLE'S BEHALF THROUGH PRAYER.   www.PrayerPups.com

PRAYER PUPS BY JEFFREY SMITH

YOU CAN READ ABOUT JESUS' BAPTISM IN MATTHEW 3:13-17, MARK 1:9-11 AND LUKE 3:21-22   www.PrayerPups.com

PRAYER PUPS BY JEFFREY SMITH

HI NIM.

CALL ME "PIM."

HUH?

IN THE BIBLE, PEOPLE'S NAMES ARE CHANGED ALL OVER THE PLACE.

SAUL BECOMES PAUL. ABRAM BECOMES ABRAHAM. SIMON IS CALLED PETER. SO I'M GOING TO BE "PIM" FROM NOW ON.

THAT'S SILLY.

SHOWS WHAT YOU KNOW, BLABBY.

ANOTHER BIG NAME CHANGE IN THE BIBLE IS JACOB, WHO BECAME ISRAEL.

www.PrayerPups.com

PRAYER PUPS BY JEFFREY SMITH

ARE YOU STILL EXERCISING MORE IN THE NEW YEAR?

NO. I'VE FALLEN BACK INTO OLD HABITS. LIKE JEREMIAH ASKED, "CAN A DALMATIAN CHANGE ITS SPOTS?"

I THINK WHAT JEREMIAH SAID WAS, "CAN A LEOPARD CHANGE ITS SPOTS?"

YOU KNOW MY UNCLE JEREMIAH AND HIS SAYINGS?

JEREMIAH 13:23 ASKS "CAN A LEOPARD CHANGE ITS SPOTS?"

www.PrayerPups.com

PRAYER PUPS BY JEFFREY SMITH

THE HOLY SPIRIT LED JESUS INTO THE DESERT, WHERE HE ATE ABSOLUTELY NOTHING FOR 40 DAYS.

THEN THE DEVIL TEMPTED HIM, SAYING "YOU'RE THE SON OF GOD, TURN THIS STONE INTO BREAD."

BUT JESUS SAID, "MAN DOES NOT LIVE BY BREAD ALONE."

AMEN TO THAT!

THERE'S ALSO COOKIES AND BACON AND CUPCAKES AND JELLY BEANS AND...

JESUS SAID, "MAN DOES NOT LIVE BY BREAD ALONE, BUT BY EVERY WORD OF GOD."

www.PrayerPups.com

PRAYER PUPS BY JEFFREY SMITH

CON, WHAT DOES "GRACE" MEAN?

WELL, NIM. "GRACE" IS THE STATE OF SANCTIFICATION BY GOD OR THE PERSONIFICATION OF ONE WHO IS UNDER SUCH DIVINE INFLUENCE. AND IT'S IMPORTANT TO NOTE THAT THE PRESENCE OF GRACE IS ANATHEMA TO THE COMMISSION OF SIN.

MM, HMM. I SEE. VERY INTERESTING.

ABBY, WHAT DOES "GRACE" MEAN?

"THE LORD IS GRACIOUS AND COMPASSIONATE, SLOW TO ANGER AND RICH IN LOVE." - PSALM 145:8

PRAYER PUPS BY JEFFREY SMITH

CON, WHAT'S A MANGER?

A TROUGH FOR FEEDING COWS.

AND THAT WAS BABY JESUS' BED?!!

YEP.

WEREN'T THEY AFRAID THE COWS WOULD EAT HIM?

I DON'T THINK SO. HE HAD SOME FRIENDS IN HIGH PLACES.

WE ALL HAVE FRIENDS IN HIGH PLACES WHEN WE TURN OUR LIFE OVER TO GOD.

PRAYER PUPS BY JEFFREY SMITH

OKAY. I'VE GOT THE KETCHUP, THE MUSTARD, THE SALSA, THE PICKLES, THE ONIONS AND THE CHEESE.

BUT THAT'S ONLY SIX. WHAT ARE THE OTHER FOUR?

OTHER FOUR? WHAT ARE YOU TALKING ABOUT?

I'M TRYING TO FOLLOW THE TEN CONDIMENTS.

YOU CAN READ ABOUT THE TEN COMMANDMENTS IN EXODUS CHAPTER 20.

PRAYER PUPS BY JEFFREY SMITH

GOD GIVES US ALL SPECIAL GIFTS AND CALLS US TO SERVE HIM IN OUR OWN UNIQUE WAY.

WE CAN SERVE HIM IN CHURCH, SCHOOL, OUR JOBS OR OUR DAILY LIVES. ALL WE HAVE TO DO IS WAIT FOR HIS CALL.

RING! RING!

HELLO?!

HI, ABBY. NO, I WAS JUST EXPECTING SOMEONE ELSE.

HAVE YOU HEARD GOD'S CALL? THINK ABOUT THE SPECIAL GIFTS HE'S GIVEN YOU AND LEARN TO GIVE BACK. www.PrayerPups.com

PRAYER PUPS BY JEFFREY SMITH

NOPE. CAN'T FIND ANY.

CAN'T FIND ANY WHAT?

GOOD NEWS. MY PASTOR SAYS THAT I SHOULD SPREAD THE GOOD NEWS, BUT THIS PAPER IS FULL OF NOTHING BUT BAD NEWS.

THE GOOD NEWS ISN'T IN THE NEWSPAPER. THE GOOD NEWS IS THE FACT THAT JESUS IS OUR SAVIOR. WE'RE SUPPOSED TO SPREAD THAT NEWS TO EVERYONE WE MEET.

BOY! LET ME TELL YOU, THIS PAPER COULD BENEFIT SOME SOME OF THAT GOOD NEWS.

NO DOUBT.

THE KINGDOM OF GOD IS NEAR. REPENT AND BELIEVE THE GOOD NEWS! - MARK 1:15   www.PrayerPups.com

PRAYER PUPS BY JEFFREY SMITH

WHY DIDN'T NOAH GO FISHING?

WHY?

BECAUSE HE ONLY HAD TWO WORMS! GET IT? HA! HA! HA! HA! HA!

HA! HA! HA! HEE! HEE! HEE...HA...HO... UMM...UH... ...AHEM...

WHAT'S THE MATTER, AMOS? DID SOMEBODY BURY YOUR SENSE-OF-HUMOR BONE?

"GOD HAS BROUGHT ME LAUGHTER, & EVERYONE WHO HEARS ABOUT THIS WILL LAUGH WITH ME." - GEN 21:6   www.PrayerPups.com

PRAYER PUPS BY JEFFREY SMITH

I'VE DECIDED THAT THE APOSTLE PAUL WAS VERY CHILD-LIKE.

WHY DO YOU THINK THAT?

BECAUSE HE CAVORTED TO CHRISTIANITY.

HE DIDN'T "CAVORT." HE CONVERTED TO CHRISTIANITY.

OH.

IT SOUNDS LIKE A LOT MORE FUN TO CAVORT THAN TO CONVERT, SO I'M STICKING WITH THAT.

PAUL CONVERTED TO CHRISTIANITY ON THE ROAD TO DAMASCUS.

www.PrayerPups.com

PRAYER PUPS BY JEFFREY SMITH

I AM SO STRESSED OUT, CON. I'VE JUST ABOUT REACHED THE END OF MY ROPE.

WELL, ABBY, REMEMBER THAT THROUGH ALL OF THIS, GOD WILL HELP. HE'S WALKING THIS DIFFICULT ROAD RIGHT ALONG BESIDE YOU. AND HE'LL NEVER ALLOW YOU TO GO THROUGH MORE THAN YOU'RE ABLE TO ENDURE.

I KNOW...

...BUT I DO WISH HE HAD A LITTLE LESS FAITH IN MY ABILITIES.

THANKS FOR THE IDEA, BEANY!

WHEN YOU'RE GOING THROUGH TOUGH TIMES, REMEMBER THAT GOD IS RIGHT THERE BESIDE YOU.

www.PrayerPups.com

PRAYER PUPS BY JEFFREY SMITH

Gracious is the Lord, and righteous; our God is merciful.

The Lord protects the simple; when I was brought low, He saved me.

Return, O my soul, to Your rest, for the LORD has dealt bountifully with you. For You have delivered my soul from death, my eyes from tears, my feet from stumbling.   -Psalm 116:5-9

IN OTHER WORDS... THANK GOD FOR GOD!

WE WOULD HAVE NOTHING IF NOT FOR THE BLESSINGS AND LOVE OF OUR LORD.

www.PrayerPups.com

PRAYER PUPS BY JEFFREY SMITH

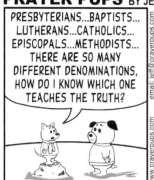
PRESBYTERIANS...BAPTISTS... LUTHERANS...CATHOLICS... EPISCOPALS...METHODISTS... THERE ARE SO MANY DIFFERENT DENOMINATIONS, HOW DO I KNOW WHICH ONE TEACHES THE TRUTH?

THAT'S EASY. AS LONG AS A CHURCH RECOGNIZES THAT JESUS IS THE SON OF GOD...

...WAS BORN OF A VIRGIN... ...DIED ON THE CROSS... ...WAS RESURRECTED THREE DAYS LATER... ...AND THAT THE ONLY WAY TO HEAVEN IS TO ACCEPT CHRIST AS YOUR SAVIOR...

...IT'S TEACHING THE RIGHT THING!

EVERYTHING ELSE IS JUST A DETAIL.

NO MATTER WHAT DENOMINATION YOU ARE, WE'RE ALL ON THE SAME SIDE...THE SIDE OF GOD!   www.PrayerPups.com

PRAYER PUPS BY JEFFREY SMITH

I TOLD A FIB YESTERDAY. BUT IT WAS JUST A LITTLE ONE. THAT'S OKAY, RIGHT?

NOPE. JAMES 2:10 SAYS THAT IF YOU STUMBLE JUST A LITTLE BIT, IT'S AS BAD AS COMMITTING ANY SIN. ALL SIN IS ONE AND THE SAME BECAUSE ALL SIN GROWS FROM US CHOOSING TO GO AHEAD AND DO WHAT GOD FORBIDS. SIN IS OUR WILLFUL SEPARATION FROM GOD.

BUT, JESUS SAVED US FROM ALL PAST AND FUTURE SINS. ASK HIS FORGIVENESS AND DON'T DO IT AGAIN.

WHAT DID YOU FIB ABOUT?

REMEMBER WHEN YOU ASKED IF I LIKED YOUR NEW COWBOY HAT?

DON'T EVER THINK OF SOMETHING AS JUST A LITTLE SIN. ALL SIN IS WRONG.   www.PrayerPups.com

PRAYER PUPS BY JEFFREY SMITH

SO PROVERBS SAYS "A GENTLE TONGUE CAN BREAK A BONE" AND YOU'RE GOING TO DEMONSTRATE?

YOU BET! OH MY GOSH, LOOK AT THAT!

WHAT IS IT?

CRUNCH!!!

TA-DAAAA!

I HOPE YOU DIDN'T BREAK A TOOTH.

YOU MEAN MY TONGUE.

SURE.

PROVERBS 25:15 USES THE TERM "GENTLE TONGUE" TO REFER TO "GENTLE SPEECH" THAT'S PERSUASIVE.   www.PrayerPups.com

PRAYER PUPS BY JEFFREY SMITH

JESUS PERFORMED THE MIRACLE AT THE REQUEST OF MARY, HIS MOTHER.

www.PrayerPups.com

PRAYER PUPS BY JEFFREY SMITH

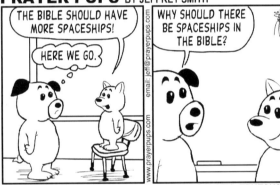

PAUL'S LETTERS WERE TO THE PEOPLE OF GALATIA, EPHESUS AND COLOSSE, NOT TO SPACE ALIENS.

www.PrayerPups.com

PRAYER PUPS BY JEFFREY SMITH

JOHN 3:16 SAYS EVERYONE WHO BELIEVES IN JESUS SHALL NOT DIE, BUT HAVE EVERLASTING LIFE.

www.PrayerPups.com

PRAYER PUPS BY JEFFREY SMITH

Panel 1: MY OWNER'S SENDING ME TO OBEDIENCE SCHOOL.

Panel 2: I'M HOPING THEY RESPECT MY FAITH AND ALLOW TIME FOR PRAYER. / THERE'S NO PRAYER IN OBEDIENCE SCHOOL.

Panel 3: OH. WELL, DO YOU THINK THEY'LL OFFER ME A "MOMENT OF SILENCE?" / IN A ROOM FULL OF DOGS?

Panel 4: I THINK YOU'LL BE REALLY LUCKY IF YOU GET EVEN A "SECOND OF SILENCE."

YOU'RE IN CONTROL OF WHEN AND WHERE YOU WANT TO PRAY...SO PRAY WHEN YOU FEEL THE URGE.

www.PrayerPups.com

PRAYER PUPS BY JEFFREY SMITH

Panel 1: DEAR DIARY-TO-GOD...

Panel 2: ...MY OWNER HAS BEEN SENDING ME TO OBEDIENCE SCHOOL...

Panel 3: ...AND IT BRINGS TO MIND THE BIBLE PASSAGE THAT SAYS, "AS OBEDIENT CHILDREN, DO NOT CONFORM TO THE EVIL DESIRES YOU HAD WHEN YOU LIVED IN IGNORANCE." WHICH PRESENTS ME WITH A DILEMMA.

Panel 4: I'M NOW AWARE THAT IT'S WRONG TO CHEW MY OWNER'S SHOES, BUT THEY JUST TASTE SO GOOD. WHAT TO DO? LOVE, ABBY

YOU SIN WHEN YOU CHOOSE TO DISOBEY GOD'S RULES. IF YOU KNOW IT'S WRONG, DON'T DO IT!

www.PrayerPups.com

PRAYER PUPS BY JEFFREY SMITH

Panel 1: YOU KNOW WHAT, JERRY? I REALLY LIKE HELPING OTHERS. / THAT'S GREAT!

Panel 2: I KNOW! IN FACT, I'D SAY I'M THE BEST PUP AROUND AT HELPING OTHER PEOPLE!

Panel 3: BE CAREFUL, NIM. YOU DON'T WANT TO BRAG. YOU SHOULD GIVE ALL THE GLORY TO GOD.

Panel 4: NO WORRIES. I'M THE BEST AT GIVING ALL THE GLORY TO GOD!

GOD WANTS US TO HELP OTHERS SO WE CAN BE MORE LIKE HIM, NOT FOR "BRAGGING RIGHTS."

www.PrayerPups.com

PRAYER PUPS BY JEFFREY SMITH

WHY DO I HAVE TO CONFESS MY SINS TO GOD. DOESN'T HE ALREADY KNOW WHAT I DID?

YES. BUT BY CONFESSING YOUR SINS, YOU ACKNOWLEDGE THAT YOU UNDERSTAND THAT YOU SINNED AGAINST <u>HIM</u>.

THE MOST IMPORTANT THING TO UNDERSTAND ABOUT SIN IS NOT HOW IT HURTS US OR THOSE AROUND US...BUT HOW IT HURTS GOD. HE LOVES US AND WANTS US TO CHOOSE HIS WAYS.

NOW I GET IT. OKAY, GET LOST! I HAVE TO TELL GOD WHAT I DID TO YOUR NEW CHEW TOY.

WHAT?

IN PSALM 32 AND 51, DAVID TELLS US THAT WE MUST ACKNOWLEDGE OUR SINS TO GOD.

www.PrayerPups.com

PRAYER PUPS BY JEFFREY SMITH

I HAVE 463 FRIENDS ON MYSPACE, 418 FRIENDS ON FACEBOOK AND 392 ON SHOUTLIFE.

I'M VERY POPULAR.

IT SOUNDS LIKE IT. HOW DID YOU GET TO KNOW THAT MANY PEOPLE?

OH, I DON'T KNOW ANY OF THEM.

THEY'RE JUST MY FRIENDS.

PROVERBS 12:26 AND 18:24 WARN THAT WE SHOULD BE CAREFUL WHO WE'RE FRIENDS WITH.

www.PrayerPups.com

PRAYER PUPS BY JEFFREY SMITH

ARE YOUR DONATIONS FOR THE NEEDY IN THAT BAG?

QUIET!!! JUST ACT NATURAL AND I'LL SLIDE THE BAG OVER TO YOU WHEN NO ONE'S LOOKING.

YOU KEEP A LOOK OUT THAT WAY. MATTHEW 6:2-4 SAYS THAT OUR GIVING SHOULD BE DONE IN SECRET. SO JUST PRETEND YOU DON'T KNOW ME.

IF ONLY THAT WERE TRUE.

HUSH, LET'S JUST DO THIS DEAL NOW!

WHEN YOU HELP OTHERS, DO IT BECAUSE IT'S WHAT GOD WANTS, NOT TO BRAG TO OTHERS.

www.PrayerPups.com

PRAYER PUPS BY JEFFREY SMITH

PSALM 27 SAYS "THE LORD IS MY LIGHT AND MY SALVATION. WHOM SHALL I FEAR?

ZOMBIES.

WHAT?

YOU SHOULD BE AFRAID OF ZOMBIES. VERY AFRAID.

FIRST OF ALL, THE PASSAGE IS TELLS ME THAT IF I TRUST IN GOD, I HAVE NOTHING TO FEAR. SECONDLY, THERE'S NO SUCH THING AS ZOMBIES.

THAT'S JUST WHAT THEY WANT YOU TO THINK.

WITH GOD ON OUR SIDE, WE SHOULD FEAR NOTHING...ESPECIALLY THINGS THAT DON'T EVEN EXIST!

www.PrayerPups.com

PRAYER PUPS BY JEFFREY SMITH

MY MINISTER SAID I SHOULD KNOW "THE WORD." WHAT WORD IS HE TALKING ABOUT?

THE BIBLE.

I ALREADY KNOW THE WORD "BIBLE."

NO, THE WORD IS IN THE BIBLE.

THERE ARE LOTS OF WORDS IN THE BIBLE

LET'S START OVER. THE BIBLE IS THE WORD AS A WHOLE.

THERE'S A HOLE IN THE BIBLE NEAR THE WORD?

THE WORD IS "RUTABAGA."

THANK YOU. WAS THAT REALLY SO HARD?

"THE WORD" MEANS THE BIBLE, OR "THE WORD OF GOD." IT'S NOT A SECRET WORD YOU HAVE TO LOOK FOR.   www.PrayerPups.com

PRAYER PUPS BY JEFFREY SMITH

WE ALL NEED TO IMPROVE OUR WALK WITH THE LORD.

I AGREE. AND PREPARING OURSELVES BEFOREHAND CAN HELP TO MAKE THE MOST OF THAT WALK.

THAT'S VERY INSIGHTFUL, ABBY. DO WE PREPARE BY EXAMINING OUR SINFUL NATURE? OR BY SEEKING COUNSEL WITH MENTORS? OR BY PRAYING FOR GUIDANCE?

OR DO WE PREPARE BY BUYING A CUTE NEW PAIR OF SHOES?

EVERY DAY IS A NEW OPPORTUNITY TO IMPROVE YOUR WALK WITH THE LORD.

www.PrayerPups.com

PRAYER PUPS BY JEFFREY SMITH

YOUR WALK WITH THE LORD IS THE MOST IMPORTANT WALK YOU'LL EVER TAKE.

www.PrayerPups.com

PRAYER PUPS BY JEFFREY SMITH

TODAY IS A GREAT DAY TO BEGIN – OR RENEW – YOUR RELATIONSHIP WITH JESUS CHRIST.

www.PrayerPups.com

PRAYER PUPS BY JEFFREY SMITH

WALKING WITH GOD IS ABOUT THE JOURNEY AND LEARNING TO LIVE YOUR LIFE THE WAY HE WANTS FOR YOU. www.PrayerPups.com

PRAYER PUPS BY JEFFREY SMITH

MY CHURCH HAS STARTED USING VIDEO IN THE SERVICE.

THAT'S VERY POPULAR THESE DAY. HOW'S IT WORKING OUT FOR YOUR CHURCH?

IT'S OKAY...

...BUT I WISH I WAS IN CHARGE OF THE REMOTE.

MANY CHURCHES TODAY USE VIDEO TO HELP MAKE THEIR SERVICE MORE DYNAMIC FOR ITS CONGREGATION.   www.PrayerPups.com

PRAYER PUPS BY JEFFREY SMITH

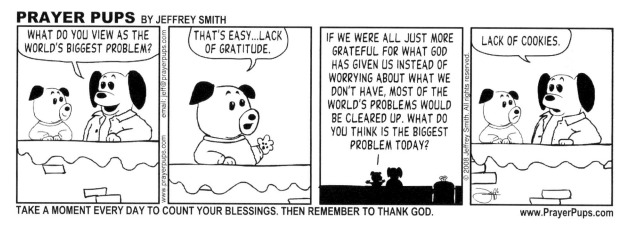

WHAT DO YOU VIEW AS THE WORLD'S BIGGEST PROBLEM?

THAT'S EASY...LACK OF GRATITUDE.

IF WE WERE ALL JUST MORE GRATEFUL FOR WHAT GOD HAS GIVEN US INSTEAD OF WORRYING ABOUT WHAT WE DON'T HAVE, MOST OF THE WORLD'S PROBLEMS WOULD BE CLEARED UP. WHAT DO YOU THINK IS THE BIGGEST PROBLEM TODAY?

LACK OF COOKIES.

TAKE A MOMENT EVERY DAY TO COUNT YOUR BLESSINGS. THEN REMEMBER TO THANK GOD.   www.PrayerPups.com

PRAYER PUPS BY JEFFREY SMITH

PAUL SAID ALL CHRISTIANS SHOULD FEEL SHAME AS LONG AS THERE ARE PEOPLE WHO HAVEN'T HEARD OF CHRIST.

WHO HASN'T HEARD OF JESUS? IN SOME COUNTRIES, PEOPLE ARE PUT TO DEATH FOR OWNING A BIBLE. THEY CAN'T TALK ABOUT JESUS.

SNIFF!

THIS IS A GOOD TIME TO PRAY FOR THOSE PEOPLE, CON.

AMEN, ABBY.

EVERY DAY, OUR BROTHERS AND SISTERS IN CHRIST SUFFER BECAUSE OF THEIR FAITH. PRAY FOR THEM.   www.PrayerPups.com

PRAYER PUPS BY JEFFREY SMITH

YOU CAN READ ABOUT MOSES AND THE ARK OF THE COVENANT IN EXODUS 25.

www.PrayerPups.com

PRAYER PUPS BY JEFFREY SMITH

JOHN 3:16 IS THE BIBLE'S DEFINING VERSE FOR ALL CHRISTIANS. IT SAYS IT ALL.

www.PrayerPups.com

PRAYER PUPS BY JEFFREY SMITH

YOU CAN READ ABOUT DAVID AND GOLIATH IN 1 SAMUEL 17. ROCK ON!

www.PrayerPups.com

PRAYER PUPS BY JEFFREY SMITH

IF YOU WANT TO BE A GOOD CHRISTIAN, YOU'VE GOT TO WORK AT IT.

SAY AMEN!

THE DEVIL STARTS EARLY, SO YOU HAVE TO WORK HARD EVERY DAY.

SAY AMEN!

WORK AT BEING GOOD! WORK AT BEING TRUE! WORK AT BEING THE BEST CHRISTIAN YOU CAN POSSIBLY BE!

SAY AMEN!

NOW DROP AND GIVE ME TWENTY!

SAY WHAT?

EVERY DAY IS A NEW BATTLE AGAINST EVIL FOR ALL CHRISTIANS. ASK GOD FOR HELP NOW.

www.PrayerPups.com

PRAYER PUPS BY JEFFREY SMITH

I'VE BEEN PRAYING FOR GOD TO GIVE ME A MILLION DOLLARS!

YOU'RE NOT SUPPOSED TO PRAY FOR THAT!

WHY NOT?

BECAUSE IT'S GREEDY AND SELF-CENTERED. YOU SHOULD PRAY FOR GOD TO HELP OTHER PEOPLE.

OH, I GET IT!

I NEED TO PRAY THAT GOD WILL HELP _OTHER_ PEOPLE GIVE ME A MILLION DOLLARS!

TO LIVE LIKE JESUS MEANS TO PUT OTHER PEOPLE'S NEEDS AHEAD OF OUR OWN SELFISH DESIRES.

www.PrayerPups.com

PRAYER PUPS BY JEFFREY SMITH

YOU KNOW CON, I REALLY DON'T LIKE TO DO WORK.

BE CAREFUL, NIM. IDLE HANDS ARE THE DEVIL'S PLAYGROUND.

NOT MUCH BUT DIRT ON THAT PLAYGROUND, HUH?

PROVERBS 14:23 SAYS, "ALL HARD WORK BRINGS A PROFIT, BUT MERE TALK LEADS ONLY TO POVERTY."

www.PrayerPups.com

PRARER PUPS BY JEFFREY SMITH

I'VE BEEN HAVING A ROUGH TIME LATELY. WHY IS GOD LETTING THIS HAPPEN?

ISAIAH & I PETER SPEAK OF BELIEVERS IN TERMS OF <u>GOLD</u>, WHICH IS "TRIED" BY FIRE TO BECOME PURE. LIKEWISE, <u>PEOPLE</u> BECOME PURE BY BEING "TRIED."

BUT YOU SHOULD ALWAYS REMEMBER THAT SOME OF GOD'S GREATEST BLESSINGS CAN ONLY COME FROM HARD TIMES. CHARLES STANLEY CALLS THEM THE "THE BLESSINGS OF BROKENNESS."

MY BLESSINGS ARE GOING TO BREAK ME?

READ ABOUT GOD REFINING US AS GOLD IN ISAIAH 1:25 AND 1 PETER 1:7-9

PRARER PUPS BY JEFFREY SMITH

HAVE THINGS GOTTEN BETTER?

NOT REALLY.

WELL TRY NOT TO WORRY. YOU WON'T HAVE TO FACE ANYTHING THAT YOU CAN'T HANDLE. JUST REMEMBER THAT GOD TESTS ALL OF US FROM TIME TO TIME.

TEST?!! THERE'S GOING TO BE A TEST?!!! THIS JUST KEEPS GETTING WORSE!!! I HOPE IT'S A MULTIPLE CHOICE TEST!

WRONG KIND OF TEST.

ABBY! I NEED A TUTOR! STAT!

IF YOU'RE GOING THROUGH A HARD TIME, REMEMBER THAT GOD WILL NEVER LEAVE YOU.

PRARER PUPS BY JEFFREY SMITH

I'M WORRIED ABOUT NIM. HE'S BEEN HAVING A ROUGH TIME LATELY.

ME TOO. I HOPE HE DOESN'T GET IMPATIENT FOR GOD TO BRING THIS BAD STREAK TO AN END. I WOULDN'T WANT HIM TO TAKE MATTERS INTO HIS OWN HANDS.

YOU DO REALIZE THIS IS NIM WE'RE TALKING ABOUT?

OH MY GOSH! YOU'RE RIGHT! YOU FIND CON AND AMOS WHILE I START CALLING THE HOSPITALS!

"BAD SEASONS" IN YOUR LIFE DON'T LAST FOREVER. TRY TO LET GOD FIX EVERYTHING FOR YOU IN HIS TIME.

PRAYER PUPS BY JEFFREY SMITH

FATHER, I DON'T KNOW HOW TO MAKE IT THROUGH THIS DIFFICULT TIME.

IT'S HARD TO DEAL WITH THE BURDENS THAT I'M FACING. BUT I KNOW YOU'RE WITH ME AND THAT YOU WILL ALWAYS GIVE ME WHAT I NEED TO CARRY ON.

LIKE ALL MY FRIENDS. THANK YOU FOR THEM.

FRIENDS ARE AMONG GOD'S GREATEST GIFTS. THEY'RE THE FAMILY YOU <u>CHOOSE</u>.

www.PrayerPups.com

PRAYER PUPS BY JEFFREY SMITH

OUR CHURCH IS REALLY EXCITED ABOUT OUR BLOG.

WELL I CAN SEE WHY. YOUR CHURCH IS RIGHT ON THE CUTTING EDGE.

THIS IS JUST THE KIND OF FORWARD-THINKING THAT CAN TAKE AN EVERDAY CHURCH AND HELP IT GROW INTO A POWERHOUSE OF IDEAS FOR ITS COMMUNITY.

I KNOW. BUT I HAVE ONE QUESTION.

WHAT'S A BLOG?

CHURCHES TODAY MUST USE EVERY WAY OF COMMUNICATION AVAILABLE TO REACH THEIR CONGREGATIONS. www.PrayerPups.com

---

PRAYER PUPS BY JEFFREY SMITH

SO YOU'RE SAYING THE ANTICHRIST COULD BE ON EARTH NOW?

IT ONLY MAKES SENSE. JESUS SAID NO ONE KNOWS WHEN THE END WILL COME EXCEPT FOR GOD. NOT ANGELS, NOT EVEN THE SON. THAT INCLUDES SATAN. SO HE MUST HAVE SOMEONE READY IN EVERY GENERATION WHO CAN BECOME ANTICHRIST.

FASCINATING. I WONDER WHO IS OUT THERE RIGHT NOW, UNAWARE THAT HE MIGHT BECOME THE ULTIMATE EVIL ON EARTH.

MY MONEY'S ON WHOEVER CREATED THE "CHOKE COLLAR."

MARK 13:32 SHOWS US THE FUTILITY OF TRYING TO DETERMINE WHEN THE END WILL COME. WE CAN'T KNOW! www.PrayerPups.com

PRAYER PUPS BY JEFFREY SMITH

DON'T JUST COMPLAIN TO GOD ABOUT WHAT YOU DON'T HAVE, THANK HIM FOR WHAT YOU DO HAVE!   www.PrayerPups.com

PRAYER PUPS BY JEFFREY SMITH

EACH AND EVERY DAY WE'RE ALIVE IS A GIFT FROM GOD AND A CHANCE TO GROW CLOSER TO HIM.   www.PrayerPups.com

PRAYER PUPS BY JEFFREY SMITH

THIS IS A GOOD DAY TO PLANT A SEED IN AN UNBELIEVER'S MIND TO HELP BRING HIM OR HER TO CHRIST.   www.PrayerPups.com

PRAYER PUPS BY JEFFREY SMITH

IN 1 SAMUEL 16, THE LORD CHOSE A YOUNG MAN TO BE KING...GOD DIDN'T JUDGE A BOOK BY ITS COVER.

www.PrayerPups.com

PRAYER PUPS BY JEFFREY SMITH

TECHNOLOGY IN CHURCHES IS EXCITING, BUT DON'T LET THE "WOW FACTOR" OVERSHADOW THE MESSAGE.   www.PrayerPups.com

PRAYER PUPS BY JEFFREY SMITH

JESUS HIMSELF WAS BAPTIZED BY JOHN IN THE RIVER JORDAN.

www.PrayerPups.com

PRAYER PUPS BY JEFFREY SMITH

Panel 1: CON SAYS MY NEW IDEA IS A BAD ONE. / WHAT'S THE IDEA?

Panel 2: HIGH-DIVE BAPTISMS! / OH, MY!

Panel 3: THE PROBLEM IS THAT I DON'T KNOW IF HE MEANS "BAD" AS IN "GOOD," LIKE: THAT'S ONE BAD BIKE, DUDE! OR IF HE MEANS "BAD" AS IN "BAD," LIKE: BAD NEWS ABOUT YOUR BIKE, DUDE!

Panel 4: GOSH. IF ONLY WE COULD KNOW WHICH HE MEANT. / YOU SEE MY DILEMMA.

BAPTISM IS THE DEATH OF OUR OLD WAYS OF SIN AND OUR REBIRTH AS A CHILD OF CHRIST.

www.PrayerPups.com

PRAYER PUPS BY JEFFREY SMITH

Panel 1: JESUS THEN FED 5000 PEOPLE WITH ONLY 5 LOAVES OF BREAD AND 2 FISH.

Panel 2: IT WAS ONE OF THE GREATEST MIRACLES OF ALL TIME.

Panel 3: I'LL SAY IT WAS A MIRACLE...

Panel 4: THEY DIDN'T EVEN HAVE TUNA HELPER BACK THEN!

MIRACLES ARE THINGS THAT HAPPEN IN DEFIANCE OF PHYSICS. JESUS PERFORMED A LOT OF THEM.

www.PrayerPups.com

PRAYER PUPS BY JEFFREY SMITH

Panel 1: I GOT LOST YESTERDAY. / HOW SCARY!

Panel 2: I KNOW. AND JUST ABOUT THE TIME MY MASTER THOUGHT HE HAD LOST ME FOREVER, HE SAW ME LOOKING FOR HIM. THEN HE RAN TO ME AND HUGGED ME AND GAVE ME LOTS OF COOKIES.

Panel 3: WOW! THAT'S JUST LIKE THE PARABLE OF THE LOST SON! / YOU'RE RIGHT!

Panel 4: I'M THE PRODIGAL POODLE.

THE PARABLE OF THE LOST SON - OR PRODIGAL SON - CAN BE FOUND IN LUKE 15:11-32.

www.PrayerPups.com

PRAYER PUPS BY JEFFREY SMITH

YOU WERE DEPRESSED A WHILE BACK, NIM. ARE YOU BETTER?

YEP!

I ASKED JESUS FOR HELP, AND HE TOOK CARE OF ME.

I'M GLAD TO HEAR IT.

ME TOO. I WAS LOWER THAN A SNAKE'S BELLY CRAWLING IN A DITCH AT THE BOTTOM OF THE GRAND CANYON.

HOW LONG HAVE YOU BEEN WAITING TO USE THAT ONE?

ALL WEEK.

TURN TO JESUS WHEN YOU NEED HELP, NO MATTER HOW LOW YOU FEEL.

www.PrayerPups.com

PRAYER PUPS BY JEFFREY SMITH

SO, CON. ARE YOU READY FOR "PAW SUNDAY?"

"PAW SUNDAY?" DON'T YOU MEAN "PALM SUNDAY?"

NOPE. SEE?

WE'RE DOGS. WE DON'T HAVE PALMS.

PALM SUNDAY IS THE SUNDAY BEFORE EASTER. IT COMMEMORATES JESUS ENTERING JERUSALEM.

www.PrayerPups.com

PRAYER PUPS BY JEFFREY SMITH

SO ABBY, SINCE THERE'S AN ANTICHRIST, WILL THERE ALSO BE AN ANTI-NIM?

ANTI-NIM? WHAT IN THE WORLD WOULD AN ANTI-NIM DO?

YOU KNOW. HE'D COME ALONG AND DO EVERYTHING IN THE EXACT OPPOSITE WAY FROM ME.

SO HE WOULD BE THE "GOOD" NIM?

HEY!!!

DON'T SPEND TOO MUCH TIME THINKING ABOUT THE ANTICHRIST. FOCUS YOUR ENERGY ON CHRIST.

www.PrayerPups.com

PRAYER PUPS BY JEFFREY SMITH

HAVE YOU STARTED LEARNING YOUR LINES FOR THE BIG EASTER PLAY?

STARTED? WHY, I'VE ALREADY MEMORIZED EVERY SINGLE WORD.

I KNOW MY PART LIKE THE BACK OF MY...HEY! WHAT IS THAT? I'VE NEVER SEEN THAT BEFORE!!!

YOU'RE NOT EXACTLY FILLING ME WITH CONFIDENCE.

NO, SERIOUSLY. WHAT IS THAT? A MOLE?!

MANY CHURCHES STAGE PLAYS ABOUT EASTER, RETELLING THE STORY OF CHRIST'S RESURRECTION.

www.PrayerPups.com

PRAYER PUPS BY JEFFREY SMITH

HOW'S THE CHURCH'S EASTER PLAY COMING ALONG, ABBY?

DON'T ASK! NOBODY KNOWS THEIR LINES! THE PIANO NEEDS TUNING! THE LIGHTS ARE ON THE FRITZ! AND THE PRINTER PUT THE WRONG DATE ON THE TICKETS!

RELAX. IT COULD BE WORSE.

JESUS COULD HAVE NEVER GIVEN US A REASON TO CELEBRATE EASTER AT ALL!

REMEMBER TO BE FOREVER GRATEFUL FOR GOD'S GIFT TO MAN OF JESUS CHRIST.

www.PrayerPups.com

PRAYER PUPS BY JEFFREY SMITH

IS NEXT SUNDAY EASTER?

NO. NEXT SUNDAY IS PALM SUNDAY.

I THOUGHT THIS SUNDAY WOULD BE PALM SUNDAY.

IT IS.

BUT YOU SAID NEXT SUNDAY WAS.

RIGHT. THE DAY AFTER TOMORROW IS NEXT SUNDAY.

THAT'S THIS SUNDAY. THE NEXT SUNDAY'S NEXT SUNDAY!

THAT'S SUNDAY AFTER NEXT!

NEVER MIND! I'LL SEE YOU IN CHURCH.

THIS SUNDAY OR NEXT SUNDAY?

WHETHER YOU CALL IT "THIS SUNDAY" OR "NEXT SUNDAY," BE SURE TO GO TO CHURCH ON SUNDAY!

www.PrayerPups.com

PRAYER PUPS BY JEFFREY SMITH

JESUS RODE INTO JERUSALEM ON A DONKEY. THE PEOPLE WAVED PALM FRONDS AT HIM AS THEY CHEERED HIS ARRIVAL.

AND ONLY FIVE DAYS LATER, THE CROWDS TURNED ON HIM AND HE WAS CRUCIFIED.

WHAT CAN WE LEARN FROM THIS STORY, NIM?

IF SOMEONE WAVES PALM FRONDS AT YOU, RUN THE OTHER WAY!

TOMORROW IS PALM SUNDAY. IT'S A SPECIAL DAY FOR CHRISTIANS AND IT KICKS OFF A SPECIAL WEEK.   www.PrayerPups.com

PRAYER PUPS BY JEFFREY SMITH

WHAT ARE YOU DOING?
THE ARK OF THE COVENANT DANCE!

WHEN THE ARK WAS DELIVERED TO THE TEMPLE, KING DAVID DANCED LIKE CRAZY IN PRAISE TO GOD.

IT'S A LOT OF FUN. WANT TO JOIN ME?
MAYBE...

WHAT WOULD OFFER GOD MORE PRAISE? THE CABBAGE PATCH OR THE FRUG?

IF ONLY EVERYONE'S LOVE OF GOD WAS SO PURE AND EXCITING THAT WE ALL DANCED LIKE FOOLS FOR HIM.   www.PrayerPups.com

PRAYER PUPS BY JEFFREY SMITH

WHAT'S WITH THE JAMS?
IT'S SPRING BREAK, BUD!

TIME TO PARTY! WHOO-HOO!
PAR-TAAAAYYYYY!

IT'S ALSO THE MOST HOLY WEEK OF THE YEAR. TIME TO REFLECT AND GIVE PRAISE.
I'VE GOT THAT COVERED TOO!

GREAT JOB, GOD! WHOO-HOO!
PUH-RAAAAISSSE!

IT'S PERFECTLY FINE TO HAVE FUN THIS WEEK, BUT DON'T FORGET WHAT THE WEEK IS REALLY ABOUT.   www.PrayerPups.com

PRAYER PUPS BY JEFFREY SMITH

AMOS' PASTOR MEANT HE SHOULD FINISH "IMPORTANT THINGS." MAKE SURE YOUR PURSUITS ARE FOR GOD.   www.PrayerPups.com

PRAYER PUPS BY JEFFREY SMITH

TOMORROW IS GOOD FRIDAY. READ THE ACCOUNT IN MATTHEW 27, MARK 15, LUKE 23 AND JOHN 19.   www.PrayerPups.com

PRAYER PUPS BY JEFFREY SMITH

www.PrayerPups.com

PRAYER PUPS BY JEFFREY SMITH

EASTER AND CHRISTMAS ARE THE TWO MOST IMPORTANT CELEBRATIONS FOR CHRISTIANS.

PRAYER PUPS BY JEFFREY SMITH

MATTHEW 28 DETAILS THE STORY OF CHRIST'S RESURRECTION. THIS IS A GOOD DAY TO READ ABOUT IT.

PRAYER PUPS BY JEFFREY SMITH

CHRIST'S GIFT WILL LIVE ON LONG AFTER THE CANDY IS JUST A FOND MEMORY.

PRAYER PUPS BY JEFFREY SMITH

ONE OF THE HOTTEST TRENDS IN CONTEMPORARY CHRISTIAN MUSIC IS REMAKING CLASSIC HYMNS.

www.PrayerPups.com

PRAYER PUPS BY JEFFREY SMITH

WITNESSING IS JUST TELLING OTHERS ABOUT YOUR WALK WITH JESUS. WITNESS TO SOMEONE TODAY!

www.PrayerPups.com

PRAYER PUPS BY JEFFREY SMITH

THE CHURCH IS A GREAT PLACE TO GET INVOLVED, BUT MAKE SURE YOU DON'T OVEREXTEND YOURSELF.

www.PrayerPups.com

PRAYER PUPS BY JEFFREY SMITH

REMEMBER TO THANK GOD FOR THE LITTLE THINGS IN LIFE THAT WE OFTEN TAKE FOR GRANTED...LIKE RAIN!   www.PrayerPups.com

PRAYER PUPS BY JEFFREY SMITH

WE DON'T NEED A SPRAY, JUST JESUS. MARK 16:17 SAYS "IN MY NAME SHALL THEY CAST OUT DEVILS."   www.PrayerPups.com

PRAYER PUPS BY JEFFREY SMITH

APRIL FOOL'S DAY CAN BE FUN, BUT MAKE SURE TO SAVE SOME TIME FOR JESUS.   www.PrayerPups.com

PRAYER PUPS BY JEFFREY SMITH

IT DOESN'T MATTER IF YOUR CHURCH IS BIG OR SMALL...AS LONG AS IT GIVES PRAISE TO JESUS.

www.PrayerPups.com

PRAYER PUPS BY JEFFREY SMITH

VISITING THE CHURCHES OF FAMILY MEMBERS HELPS ALL OF YOU GROW CLOSER.

www.PrayerPups.com

PRAYER PUPS BY JEFFREY SMITH

IT'S FUN TO STOMP ON THE DEVIL'S HEAD. TRY IT RIGHT NOW AND SEE HOW YOU FEEL!

www.PrayerPups.com

PRAYER PUPS BY JEFFREY SMITH

OUR STRENGTH COMES FROM GOD AND FROM NOWHERE ELSE.

www.PrayerPups.com

PRAYER PUPS BY JEFFREY SMITH

JUST BECAUSE YOU WANT TO LIVE BY GOD'S RULES AND STUMBLE DOESN'T MAKE YOU A HYPOCRITE!

www.PrayerPups.com

PRAYER PUPS BY JEFFREY SMITH

"THE FEAR OF THE LORD IS THE BEGINNING OF WISDOM." - PROVERBS 1:7

www.PrayerPups.com

PRAYER PUPS BY JEFFREY SMITH

HAVE YOU SEEN THE CHURCH'S NEW WEBSITE?

NO. IS IT NICE?

NICE? IT'S GOT A CALENDAR AND INSTANT MESSAGING AND PODCASTS AND STREAMING VIDEO AND GAMES AND NEWS AND SUB-SITES FOR EACH SUNDAY SCHOOL CLASS AND TONS OF PICTURES AND A FACEBOOK APP AND TOTALLY INTERACTIVE AREAS THAT KEEP EVERYONE UP-TO-DATE CONSTANTLY ON EVERY MINUTE DETAIL OF THE CHURCH AND ITS STAFF SEVEN DAYS A WEEK!

WOW! THAT SOUNDS INCREDIBLE!

YEAH. TOO BAD I CAN'T FIGURE OUT HOW TO USE IT.

IF YOUR CHURCH'S WEBSITE DOESN'T COMMUNICATE WITH THE CONGREGATION, IT'S NOT DOING ITS JOB.   www.PrayerPups.com

PRAYER PUPS BY JEFFREY SMITH

DID YOU KNOW THAT ISAAC'S NAME MEANS "LAUGHTER."

MM-HMM.

THAT'S A REALLY FUNNY NAME... "LAUGHTER."

MM-HMM.

I MEAN, TO NAME A KID SOMETHING LIKE "LAUGHTER IS REALLY ODD. IT'S NOT A NAME YOU HEAR EVERYDAY.

MM-HMM.

I WONDER WHAT "NIM" MEANS.

I DON'T KNOW. "PEST," MAYBE?

ABRAHAM MEANS "FATHER OF NATIONS," ISAAC MEANS "LAUGHTER," & JACOB MEANS "HELD BY THE HEEL."   www.PrayerPups.com

PRAYER PUPS BY JEFFREY SMITH

IF GOD LOVES ME SO MUCH, HOW COME I'M NOT RICH?

GOD'S NOT SOME BIG LOTTERY IN THE SKY. HE KNOWS YOUR HEART. IF YOU LOVE MONEY MORE THAN YOU LOVE HIM, HE MIGHT MAKE YOU STRUGGLE IN ORDER TO GROW CLOSER TO HIM.

SO YOU'RE SAYING I'M NOT RICH BECAUSE HE LOVES ME?

MAYBE.

TOUCHÉ, GOD.

TAKE A MOMENT TO REASSESS YOUR LIFE TO MAKE SURE GOD IS NUMBER 1. THEN READ MARK 10:17-27.   www.PrayerPups.com

40 - Prayer Pups | Four Panels

PRAYER PUPS BY JEFFREY SMITH

WHY DID GOD MAKE ALL THE HEALTHY FOOD TASTE SO BAD?

WHAT ARE YOU TALKING ABOUT? BROCCOLI IS GOOD FOR YOU AND IT'S DELICIOUS!

BROCCOLI?! BLEEECCCCCHHHH!!!

BE CAREFUL. YOUR FACE MIGHT FREEZE LIKE THAT.

MAKE ME EAT BROCCOLI AND IT PROBABLY WILL!

WOULDN'T IT BE GREAT IF BROCCOLI TASTED LIKE CHOCOLATE CHIP ICE CREAM?

www.PrayerPups.com

PRAYER PUPS BY JEFFREY SMITH

I HAVE A ROUTINE EVERY DAY.

WHAT IS IT?

I JUMP OUT OF BED BEFORE THE ALARM GOES OFF. TAKE A BIG DRINK OF WATER AND SHOUT, "GOOD MORNING, LORD!"

I HAVE A SIMILAR ROUTINE.

I JUMP OUT OF BED AND REACH TO TURN THE ALARM OFF, BUT KNOCK MY WATER OVER INSTEAD AND SHOUT, "GOOD LORD, IS IT MORNING ALREADY?"

WE SHOULD GREET EACH DAY AS A GIFT FROM OUR LOVING GOD.

www.PrayerPups.com

PRAYER PUPS BY JEFFREY SMITH

MY FRIEND IS REALLY SICK AND HAD TO GO TO THE HOSPITAL.

OH, NO!

SHE'S FACING ROUGH TIMES. BUT HER DOCTORS ARE THE BEST AROUND, SO SHE'S IN GOOD HANDS.

DID YOU PRAY FOR HER?

A LOT!

THEN SHE'S IN THE BEST HANDS AROUND!

WHEN SOMEONE YOU LOVE IS SICK, PRAY FOR THEM, THEIR FAMILIES, THEIR DOCTORS.

www.PrayerPups.com

PRAYER PUPS BY JEFFREY SMITH

OBEDIENCE OF GOD IS THE PUREST CONFESSION OF FAITH WE CAN MAKE.

www.PrayerPups.com

PRAYER PUPS BY JEFFREY SMITH

STOP FIGHTING FOR WHAT YOU WANT AND START LISTENING TO WHAT GOD WANTS FOR YOU.

www.PrayerPups.com

PRAYER PUPS BY JEFFREY SMITH

IS YOUR PRAYER TIME A FELLOWSHIP WITH GOD, OR DO YOU JUST WHINE AND BEG?

www.PrayerPups.com

PRAYER PUPS BY JEFFREY SMITH

OBEDIENCE IS ONE OF THE HARDEST THINGS CHRISTIANS FACE EVERY DAY. PRAY TO GOD FOR STRENGTH.   www.PrayerPups.com

PRAYER PUPS BY JEFFREY SMITH

CARRY THIS MESSAGE OVER TO YOUR LOVED ONES. IF YOU WANT TO SHOW RESPECT, SHOW OBEDIENCE.   www.PrayerPups.com

PRAYER PUPS BY JEFFREY SMITH

GOD'S LAWS ARE ABSOLUTE. DON'T TRY TO REWRITE THEM FOR YOUR OWN PURPOSES.   www.PrayerPups.com

PRAYER PUPS BY JEFFREY SMITH

DEAR DIARY-TO-GOD... I JUST FINISHED A FULL WEEK OF OBEDIENCE CLASSES.

I LEARNED A LOT AND NOW MY MASTER THINKS I'M THE PERFECT PUP.

BUT I'LL STILL PROBABLY MAKE MISTAKES. AFTER ALL, I'M ONLY CANINE. BUT EVEN WHEN I DO, SHE'LL FORGIVE ME BECAUSE SHE'S OBEDIENT TO YOU.

I GUESS EVERYONE'S OBEDIENT TO SOMEONE, HUH? WELL, TA FOR NOW! LOVE, ABBY

DON'T BEGRUDGE THE PEOPLE YOU'RE SUPPOSED TO OBEY. LOVE THEM, LOVE GOD AND DO YOUR DUTY.   www.PrayerPups.com

PRAYER PUPS BY JEFFREY SMITH

OUR PASTOR ASKED US IF WE KNEW "OUR WAY HOME."

SO I SAID, "DUH. NOT ONLY DO I KNOW MY WAY HOME, BUT I KNOW WHERE YOU LIVE TOO, PASTOR! IN FACT, I'M QUITE FOND OF THAT FIRE HYDRANT IN YOUR FRONT YARD."

OH, NIM, YOU DIDN'T!   YEP, I DID.

DID YOU KNOW A PREACHER'S FACE TURNS PURPLE BEFORE IT TURNS RED?

WHEN A PREACHER SPEAKS OF "FINDING YOUR WAY HOME," HE MEANS "YOUR ETERNAL HOME IN HEAVEN."   www.PrayerPups.com

PRAYER PUPS BY JEFFREY SMITH

WE LEARNED THE STORY OF ESTHER IN CHURCH YESTERDAY.

BOY, YOUR CHURCH IS REALLY BEHIND THE TIMES!

BEHIND THE TIMES? WHAT DO YOU MEAN?

ESTHER WAS LAST MONTH! DON'T YOU REMEMBER ALL THE EGGS?

ESTHER IS ONE OF THE MOST GRIPPING BOOKS OF THE BIBLE. IF YOU HAVEN'T READ IT, READ IT NOW.   www.PrayerPups.com

PRAYER PUPS BY JEFFREY SMITH

IF THIS DOESN'T MAKE SENSE TO YOU, MAYBE IT'S TIME FOR A NEW WEBSITE FOR YOUR CHURCH!

PRAYER PUPS BY JEFFREY SMITH

C.S. LEWIS USED HIS IMAGINATION AND GIFT OF WRITING TO SPREAD THE WORD OF JESUS CHRIST.

PRAYER PUPS BY JEFFREY SMITH

JESUS WAS BAPTIZED IN THE RIVER JORDAN BY JOHN THE BAPTIST.

PRAYER PUPS BY JEFFREY SMITH

VOLUNTEER FOR SOMETHING AT YOUR CHURCH THIS WEEK. THEN DO WHATEVER YOU'RE ASKED TO DO.   www.PrayerPups.com

PRAYER PUPS BY JEFFREY SMITH

WHATEVER YOUR SPECIAL TALENT IS, YOUR CHURCH NEEDS IT. SO GET IN THE GAME!   www.PrayerPups.com

PRAYER PUPS BY JEFFREY SMITH

DEFENDING YOUR FAITH IS A DAILY BATTLE. PRACTICE TELLING YOUR STORY OF FAITH TODAY.   www.PrayerPups.com

PRAYER PUPS BY JEFFREY SMITH

DON'T BE AFRAID TO TELL OTHERS ABOUT YOUR RELATIONSHIP WITH JESUS.

PRAYER PUPS BY JEFFREY SMITH

NIM'S APPROACH IS THE WRONG WAY TO BRING PEOPLE TO JESUS.

PRAYER PUPS BY JEFFREY SMITH

THE WHOLE POINT OF APOLOGETICS IS TO WIN SOULS FOR CHRIST...NOT TO WIN AN ARGUMENT.

PRAYER PUPS BY JEFFREY SMITH

PRAY FOR YOUR COUNTRY, MILITARY, MEDIA, BUSINESS, EDUCATION, CHURCH AND FAMILY.

www.**PrayerPups**.com

PRAYER PUPS BY JEFFREY SMITH

WHO AND WHAT DID YOU PRAY FOR YESTERDAY? MAKE SURE TO KEEP THE PRAYERS GOING TODAY.

www.**PrayerPups**.com

PRAYER PUPS BY JEFFREY SMITH

FIND OUT WHAT YOUR CHURCH HAS PLANNED THIS MONTH AND GET INVOLVED!

www.**PrayerPups**.com

PRAYER PUPS BY JEFFREY SMITH

YOU CAN ALWAYS TALK TO GOD. 24 HOURS A DAY. 7 DAYS A WEEK. 365 DAYS A YEAR.

www.PrayerPups.com

PRAYER PUPS BY JEFFREY SMITH

OUR FRIENDS IN MEXICO CELEBRATE THE FIFTH OF MAY AS A DAY OF VICTORY.

www.PrayerPups.com

PRAYER PUPS BY JEFFREY SMITH

DON'T BELIEVE EVERYTHING YOU'RE TOLD.

www.PrayerPups.com

PRAYER PUPS BY JEFFREY SMITH

THE PENTECOST IS ONE OF THE MOST IMPORTANT EVENTS IN OUR HISTORY.

www.PrayerPups.com

PRAYER PUPS BY JEFFREY SMITH

SOME CHURCHES ARE TRADITIONAL, SOME ARE CONTEMPORARY. FIND ONE THAT FITS YOU.

www.PrayerPups.com

PRAYER PUPS BY JEFFREY SMITH

DOES YOUR CHURCH GET THINGS DONE OR DOES IT SPEND TIME PREPARING TO GET THINGS DONE?

www.PrayerPups.com

PRAYER PUPS BY JEFFREY SMITH

HOW GOES THE COMMITTEE ON COMMITTEES?

THEY'VE PUT ME ON A NEW TASK FORCE.

WHAT'S THE NEW TASK FORCE CHARGED WITH DOING?

WE HAVE TO CREATE A SMALL GROUP COUNCIL THAT WILL MAKE RECOMMENDATIONS TO MY TASK FORCE ON HOW TO BETTER STRUCTURE OUR COMMITTEES, WHICH I WILL FORMALLY PRESENT TO THE COMMITTEE ON COMMITTEES.

THAT MAKES MY BRAIN HURT!

TELL ME ABOUT IT.

THE FEWER LAYERS OF BUREAUCRACY IN YOUR CHURCH, THE MORE TIME TO GET THINGS DONE. www.PrayerPups.com

PRAYER PUPS BY JEFFREY SMITH

I'M WORRIED ABOUT WHERE MY NEXT MEAL WILL COME FROM.

THAT'S SILLY. YOUR MASTER WILL ALWAYS FEED YOU.

BESIDES, MATTHEW 6:26 SAYS, "LOOK AT THE BIRDS OF THE AIR; THEY DO NOT SOW OR REAP OR STORE AWAY IN BARNS, AND YET YOUR HEAVENLY FATHER FEEDS THEM. ARE YOU NOT MUCH MORE VALUABLE THAN THEY?

I DIDN'T HEAR ANYTHING ABOUT EUKANUBA IN THAT VERSE.

IF YOU PURSUE A RELATIONSHIP WITH GOD ABOVE MATERIAL THINGS, HE WILL TAKE CARE OF YOUR NEEDS. www.PrayerPups.com

PRAYER PUPS BY JEFFREY SMITH

WHY DOES THE SONG "OUR GOD IS AN AWESOME GOD" SAY "HE RAINS FROM HEAVEN ABOVE?"

I MEAN, THAT'S NOT VERY HIGH PRAISE TO SAY THAT GOD JUST GETS US ALL WET!

IT'S NOT RAIN, LIKE R-A-I-N, YOU GOOF. IT'S REIGN, LIKE R-E-I-G-N.

SPELL IT HOWEVER YOU WANT.

BUT I'VE BEEN AROUND THE DOGPARK ENOUGH TIMES TO KNOW THAT SOMEONE'S GETTING WET!

OUR GOD IS AN AWESOME GOD. TELL SOMEONE YOU MEET ABOUT HIM TODAY! www.PrayerPups.com

PRAYER PUPS BY JEFFREY SMITH

TELL ME A BIBLE STORY, NIM.

OKAY. A-HEM!

JESUS TOLD HIS APOSTLES TO GO OUT AND MAKE DISCIPLES OF ALL NATIONS, BAPTIZING THEM IN THE NAME OF THE FATHER AND OF THE SON AND OF THE HOLY SPIRIT. BUT THOMAS RAISED HIS HAND AND ASKED, "WHAT DO WE GET OUT OF THIS?"

AND JESUS SAID, "7 PERCENT ON A SLIDING SCALE."

WHAT THE...

AND THAT'S WHAT'S KNOWN AS "THE GREAT COMMISSION."

IT IS NOT!

THE GREAT COMMISSION SAYS THAT ALL CHRISTIANS MUST SPREAD GOD'S WORD THROUGHOUT THE WORLD.   www.PrayerPups.com

PRAYER PUPS BY JEFFREY SMITH

CON, DO YOU THINK JESUS EVER COMPETED IN THE OLYMPICS?

THE BIBLE DOESN'T MENTION IT, BUT I DON'T THINK SO.

HE ONLY HAD THREE YEARS IN HIS ENTIRE MINISTRY, SO HE DIDN'T HAVE A LOT OF TIME FOR SPORTS.

TOO BAD! HE COULD HAVE WON THE 400 METER TRACK AND SWIMMING EVENTS AT THE SAME TIME BY RUNNING ON TOP OF THE WATER!

PRAY FOR THE OLYMPIC ATHLETES.   www.PrayerPups.com

PRAYER PUPS BY JEFFREY SMITH

IT'S ALMOST SUMMER!

I KNOW.

THAT MEANS BAR-BE-CUES, SWIMMING, STAYING OUTSIDE LATER, SHORTS, SANDALS, GOING TO THE BEACH, VACATION, NO SCHOOL!

YOU FORGOT THE MOST IMPORTANT THING.

WHAT'S THAT?

VACATION BIBLE SCHOOL!

VACATION BIBLE SCHOOL IS A GREAT WAY TO LEARN ABOUT JESUS...AND HAVE A LOT OF FUN, TO BOOT!   www.PrayerPups.com

PRAYER PUPS BY JEFFREY SMITH

CON, HAVE YOU EVER BEEN TO THE HOLY LAND?

NO, BUT I'D SURE LIKE TO GO!

ME TOO!

YOU KNOW IT'S CALLED "THE LAND OF MILK AND HONEY."

I KNOW, BUT I'M HOPING THEY HAVE SOME PEANUT BUTTER AND BREAD, TOO.

IN EXODUS 3:8, GOD PROMISES TO DELIVER THE JEWS INTO "A LAND FLOWING WITH MILK AND HONEY."

PRAYER PUPS BY JEFFREY SMITH

EVER FEEL DEPRESSED AND YOU DON'T KNOW WHY?

WHEN YOU DO, READ PSALM 42:11 OUT LOUD TO YOURSELF.

Why are you downcast, O my soul? Why so disturbed within me? Put your hope in God, for I will yet praise Him, my Savior and my God.

-Psalm 42:11

THEN, WHEN YOUR SOUL FEELS BETTER, YOU'LL FEEL BETTER!

COMBINE PSALM 42:11 AND THE LORD'S PRAYER FOR DOUBLE SHOT OF "FEEL GOOD!"

PRAYER PUPS BY JEFFREY SMITH

I'M NOW TOTALLY BRILLIANT!

HUH?

JAMES 1:5 SAYS "IF ANY OF YOU LACKS WISDOM, HE SHOULD ASK GOD...AND IT WILL BE GIVEN TO HIM."

I ASKED, THEREFORE I'M NOW A TRUE BRANIAC!

DON'T YOU THINK YOU'RE BEING A LITTLE...

SILENCE! I FEEL A THOUGHT COMING ON!

WHEN THE BIBLE SPEAKS OF WISDOM, IT USUALLY MEANS WISDOM ABOUT GOD AND SALVATION.

PRAYER PUPS BY JEFFREY SMITH

WE SHOULDN'T WORRY ABOUT WHAT WE DON'T HAVE...WE SHOULD GIVE THANKS FOR WHAT WE DO HAVE!

www.PrayerPups.com

PRAYER PUPS BY JEFFREY SMITH

SUMMER IS A GREAT TIME TO CATCH UP ON THE DVD MOVIES YOU'VE BEEN WANTING TO SEE!

www.PrayerPups.com

PRAYER PUPS BY JEFFREY SMITH

DEUTERONOMY 8:1-3 HELPS US UNDERSTAND HOW TO LIVE GODLY LIVES.

www.PrayerPups.com

PRAYER PUPS BY JEFFREY SMITH

ABBY, HELP ME WORK ON MY JOURNALISM SKILLS BY TELLING ME ABOUT JONAH AND THE WHALE.

OKAY, ONE DAY JONAH... WHO? JONAH. AND A WHALE.... WHAT? A WHALE... WHERE? UMM... WHEN? WHY? HEY!

WELL, I THINK THAT COVERS JUST ABOUT EVERYTHING. SO WHY DO I FEEL LIKE I'VE FORGOTTEN SOMETHING?

KEEP IT UP, AND I'LL MAKE YOU FORGET SOMETHING!

HOW?

YOU CAN READ ABOUT JONAH AND THE WHALE IN JONAH 1 AND 2.

www.PrayerPups.com

PRAYER PUPS BY JEFFREY SMITH

ARE YOU DOING ANYTHING SPECIAL THIS WEEKEND?

MY SUNDAY SCHOOL CLASS IS GOING TO THE BEACH.

THAT SOUNDS LIKE A LOT OF FUN!

OH, YEAH. PINK SKIN... FIVE HOURS OF SUN... LET THE PARTY BEGIN!

HAVE A SAFE AND RESTFUL WEEKEND!

www.PrayerPups.com

PRAYER PUPS BY JEFFREY SMITH

MY EYES DON'T LOOK HAUGHTY, DO THEY?

HUH?

I'M READING PSALM 131. I'VE MADE SURE MY HEART'S NOT PROUD...

I DON'T CONCERN MYSELF WITH GREAT MATTERS AND I'VE PUT MY HOPE IN THE LORD. BUT I NEED TO MAKE SURE MY EYES AREN'T HAUGHTY.

NOPE. NOT HAUGHTY. THEY'RE A LITTLE BLOODSHOT. AND YOU'VE GOT SOME CRUST IN THE CORNERS.

HEY!!!

PSALM 131 SHOWS US THAT WE SHOULDN'T JUDGE OTHERS. JUDGMENT IS TO BE LEFT TO GOD.

www.PrayerPups.com

PRAYER PUPS BY JEFFREY SMITH

PROVERBS 6:16-19 TELLS US 6 THINGS THE LORD HATES, 7 WHICH ARE AN ABOMINATION TO HIM.

www.PrayerPups.com

PRAYER PUPS BY JEFFREY SMITH

THE SHEDDING OF INNOCENT BLOOD IS AN ABOMINATION TO GOD.

www.PrayerPups.com

PRAYER PUPS BY JEFFREY SMITH

THE 4TH THING PROVERBS 6:16-19 TELLS US THAT GOD HATES IS "A HEART THAT DEVISES WICKED SCHEMES."   www.PrayerPups.com

PRAYER PUPS BY JEFFREY SMITH

FEET THAT ARE QUICK TO RUSH TO EVIL BETRAY A HEART THAT SECRETLY DWELLS IN DARK PLACES.

PRAYER PUPS BY JEFFREY SMITH

THE SIXTH THING THE LORD HATES IS "A FALSE WITNESS WHO POURS OUT LIES."

PRAYER PUPS BY JEFFREY SMITH

"THERE ARE SIX THINGS THE LORD HATES, SEVEN THAT ARE DETESTABLE TO HIM" - PROVERBS 6:16-19

PRAYER PUPS BY JEFFREY SMITH

CON'S BIG BIBLE FACTS

THE BOOK OF **ISAIAH**

ISAIAH 49:16 WILL ROCK YOUR SOCKS OFF!!!

IT FEATURES GOD TELLING THE PEOPLE OF ISRAEL HE WILL NEVER FORGET THEM, SAYING, "I HAVE ENGRAVED YOU ON THE PALMS OF MY HANDS..."

NOW...WHAT PROOF DID JESUS OFFER HIS DISCIPLES THAT HE HAD RETURNED FROM THE DEAD? THE HOLES IN HIS PALMS. THOSE HOLES WERE A SYMBOL OF GOD'S LOVE AND THE FACT THAT HE WILL NEVER FORGET US.

AND WHAT'S COOL IS THAT ISAIAH WAS WRITTEN 700 YEARS BEFORE JESUS!

YOU COULD SAY THAT THE HOLES IN JESUS' HANDS REPRESENT THE NAMES OF THOSE HE DIED FOR.

www.PrayerPups.com

PRAYER PUPS BY JEFFREY SMITH

MY CHURCH HAD SIX BAPTISMS THIS PAST SUNDAY.

THAT'S AWESOME! YOU KNOW, EVERY TIME MY CHURCH GOES THROUGH ONE OF OUR RITUALS, I CAN ACTUALLY FEEL MY RELATIONSHIP WITH GOD GROW. IT STRENGTHENS MY FAITH AND HELPS ME TO BECOME AN ACTIVE PART OF THE "BODY OF CHRIST."

HOW DID THE BAPTISMS MAKE YOU FEEL, AMOS?

HUNGRY! WE WERE 30 MINUTES LATE GETTING OUT OF CHURCH!

MAKE SURE YOU'RE INVOLVED IN YOUR CHURCH'S RITUALS AND NOT JUST "GOING THROUGH THE MOTIONS." www.PrayerPups.com

---

PRAYER PUPS BY JEFFREY SMITH

IN GALATIANS, PAUL TALKS ABOUT THE FRUITS OF THE SPIRIT.

THEY'RE THE NINE GIFTS GIVEN TO US BY GOD THAT HELP US BECOME BETTER PEOPLE: LOVE, JOY, PEACE, PATIENCE, KINDNESS, GOODNESS, FAITHFULNESS, GENTLENESS AND SELF-CONTROL.

THAT'S COOL! YOU NEED TO TELL EVERYONE ABOUT THIS!

IT'S NOT REALLY A SECRET.

COME HERE ABBY! CON'S TALKING ABOUT THE HOLY VEGETABLES!

YOU CAN READ ABOUT THE FRUITS OF THE SPIRIT IN GALATIANS 5:22. www.PrayerPups.com

PRAYER PUPS BY JEFFREY SMITH

YOU CAN FIND OUT ABOUT THE FRUITS OF THE SPIRIT IN GALATIANS 5.

www.PrayerPups.com

PRAYER PUPS BY JEFFREY SMITH

BE PATIENT, IT TAKES TIME FOR THE FRUITS OF THE HOLY SPIRIT TO GROW WITHIN YOU.

www.PrayerPups.com

PRAYER PUPS BY JEFFREY SMITH

LACK OF GRATITUDE IS ONE OF THE BIGGEST PROBLEMS IN THE WORLD TODAY.

www.PrayerPups.com

PRAYER PUPS BY JEFFREY SMITH

FINDING GOD IS EVEN EASIER THAN USING A SEARCH ENGINE.

www.PrayerPups.com

PRAYER PUPS BY JEFFREY SMITH

"YOU CREATED ALL THINGS, AND BY YOUR WILL THEY WERE CREATED AND HAVE THEIR BEING." - REV. 4:11   www.PrayerPups.com

---

PRAYER PUPS BY JEFFREY SMITH

TRUST IN THE LORD TO FULFILL ALL YOUR NEEDS AND DESIRES.

www.PrayerPups.com

PRAYER PUPS BY JEFFREY SMITH

I HEARD A MAN COMPLAIN ABOUT THE PRICE OF GAS TODAY. HE SAID IT WAS AN OUTRAGE HOW MUCH HE HAD TO PAY.

BUT GAS WAS NOT THE ONLY THING HE LIKED TO RAVE ABOUT.

HE THEN SAID HIS GROCERY BILL WAS REALLY TOO FAR OUT.

IN SPITE OF ALL HIS BLESSINGS, NO GRATITUDE HAD HE. HE FAILED TO RECOGNIZE...

THAT PRAYER IS STILL FREE!

IF YOU'RE FEELING BEATEN DOWN BY THE HIGH COST OF LIVING, MAKE A DATE FOR PRAYER TIME WITH GOD.   www.PrayerPups.com

PRAYER PUPS BY JEFFREY SMITH

I WANT MY MASTER TO DYE MY FUR.

I WANT SOME OF IT RED, SOME BLUE, SOME PINK AND MAYBE EVEN SOME CHARTREUSE!

WHY IN THE WORLD WOULD YOU WANT TO DO THAT, NIM?

THEN I COULD BE LIKE JOSEPH AND HAVE A COAT OF MANY COLORS!

JOSEPH'S BROTHERS WERE ENVIOUS OF HIS COAT OF MANY COLORS.   www.PrayerPups.com

PRAYER PUPS BY JEFFREY SMITH

CON, WHY DO SOME PEOPLE CONTINUE TO MAKE THE SAME MISTAKES?

IT'S JUST IN THEIR NATURE, I GUESS.

PROVERBS 26:11 SAYS, "AS A DOG RETURNS TO ITS VOMIT, SO A FOOL REPEATS HIS FOLLY."

EEEEWWWW!

DON'T KEEP TRYING TO DO THE SAME THINGS THAT HAVE FAILED IN THE PAST, START ANEW WITH JESUS!   www.PrayerPups.com

PRAYER PUPS BY JEFFREY SMITH

IT IS SO HOT OUTSIDE! I'M BURNING UP!

WHY IS GOD MAKING ME SO HOT THIS SUMMER?

GOD'S ALREADY TAKEN CARE OF YOU. HE MADE IT SO THAT WHEN A DOG GETS HOT, HE PANTS. WHY DON'T YOU TRY THAT?

I DON'T HAVE ANY PANTS.

GOD KNOWS EVERYTHING WE NEED BEFORE WE NEED IT.

www.PrayerPups.com

PRAYER PUPS BY JEFFREY SMITH

MY FRIEND SAID IT'S OKAY FOR CHRISTIANS TO SIN BECAUSE GOD'S FORGIVENESS IS LIKE A FREE PASS TO DO WHATEVER YOU WANT.

YOUR FRIEND IS WRONG. AND IF HE THINKS THAT WAY, HE MIGHT NOT HAVE SINCERELY ACCEPTED CHRIST.

IT'S FUNNY. THAT'S _EXACTLY_ WHAT I TOLD HIM!

ACTUALLY, I JUST SAID "SHUT UP, YOU POOTYHEAD!" BUT THE GIST WAS THE SAME AS WHAT YOU SAID.

GOD'S FORGIVENESS THROUGH CHRIST ISN'T A "GET OUT OF JAIL FREE" CARD FOR US.

www.PrayerPups.com

PRAYER PUPS BY JEFFREY SMITH

MY MASTER IS WORKING HARD PREPARING FOR A PARTY FOR HER SUNDAY SCHOOL CLASS.

SHE'S BEEN COOKING, BAKING, MIXING, MOPPING, DUSTING, VACUUMING, POLISHING THE SILVER, HANGING PICTURES, BLEACHING THE WALKWAYS, TESTING RECIPES, FINDING JUST THE RIGHT CANDLES, BAKING PIES, ADDRESSING INVITATIONS...

I THOUGHT A PARTY WAS A PIZZA AND A MOVIE FROM THE VIDEO STORE.

NO! IT'S A _GIRLS'_ PARTY!

PREPARING FOR GUESTS SHOWS THEM HOW MUCH THEY MEAN TO YOU.

www.PrayerPups.com

PRAYER PUPS BY JEFFREY SMITH

I TOOK A CORRESPONDENCE COURSE IN SPEED READING AND READ THE ENTIRE BIBLE IN 32 MINUTES...FLAT!

WOW! DID YOU RETAIN MUCH?

I WON'T KNOW UNTIL NEXT WEEK.

THAT'S WHEN MY RETENTION COURSE ARRIVES.

DON'T RUSH THROUGH THE BIBLE. TAKE YOUR TIME SO YOU CAN ABSORB THE TRUTH.

PRAYER PUPS BY JEFFREY SMITH

I HATE GOING TO THE VET! I HATE IT! I HATE IT! I HATE IT!!!

YOU SHOULD TRY TO CHANGE YOUR PERSPECTIVE.

TRY TO HAVE GRATITUDE THAT GOD HAS PROVIDED US WITH MODERN MEDICINE. INSTEAD OF SAYING "I HATE THE VET!" SAY "THANK YOU, GOD, FOR CREATING TALENTED VETERINARIANS I CAN GO TO."

EASY FOR YOU TO SAY. YOU DON'T HAVE TO GO TO THE VET TODAY.

TRUE.

SOMETIMES IT'S HARD TO REMEMBER TO GIVE THANKS FOR THINGS THAT AREN'T FUN. TRY TO DO IT ANYWAY.

PRAYER PUPS BY JEFFREY SMITH

I HAVE AN IDEA THAT'S GONNA MAKE MILLIONS!

WHAT IS IT?

I'M GONNA MAKE A BUNCH OF PRODUCTS THAT ALL ASK "WHAT WOULD JESUS DO?"

ALREADY BEEN DONE.

WHAT DONE JESUS DO?

BEFORE MAKING ANY BIG DECISION, ASK YOURSELF WHAT JESUS WOULD DO.

PRAYER PUPS BY JEFFREY SMITH

THE BIBLE HAS A LOT TO TELL US. MAKE SURE YOU UNDERSTAND WHAT IT SAYS.

www.PrayerPups.com

PRAYER PUPS BY JEFFREY SMITH

HAVING A BIG PLAN IS A GREAT IDEA, BUT BE CAREFUL YOU'RE DOING IT FOR THE RIGHT REASONS.

www.PrayerPups.com

PRAYER PUPS BY JEFFREY SMITH

GOD WILL SATISFY ALL OF YOUR NEEDS.

www.PrayerPups.com

PRAYER PUPS BY JEFFREY SMITH

ONLY A FOOL RELIES ON HIMSELF OVER GOD.

PRAYER PUPS BY JEFFREY SMITH

DO YOU DO THINGS TO BRING GLORY TO GOD OR TO BRING GLORY TO YOURSELF?

PRAYER PUPS BY JEFFREY SMITH

DON'T JUST ASK GOD TO DO THINGS FOR YOU, THANK HIM FOR ALL HE'S ALREADY DONE FOR YOU.

PRAYER PUPS BY JEFFREY SMITH

SPREADING THE LOVE OF JESUS IS EVERYONE'S BUSINESS!

www.PrayerPups.com

PRAYER PUPS BY JEFFREY SMITH

DON'T THINK OF HEAVEN AS A "CONCEPT," THINK OF IT AS AN ACTUAL <u>PLACE.</u>

www.PrayerPups.com

PRAYER PUPS BY JEFFREY SMITH

HEAVEN IS A PLACE THAT GOD HAS WAITING FOR US.

www.PrayerPups.com

PRAYER PUPS BY JEFFREY SMITH

SO YOU SAY JESUS HAS PREPARED A THING FOR ME IN HEAVEN?

NO, A PLACE.

THE THING IS A PLACE?

NO, JESUS HAS PREPARED A PLACE.

TO PUT THE THING IN?

NO, TO PUT YOU IN.

I'LL BE PUT IN SOME...THING?

YOU'RE NOT LISTENING TO ME. JESUS IS PREPARING A PLACE FOR YOU. END OF STORY!

OKAY, I GET IT. NOW TELL ME MORE ABOUT THE THING.

JESUS HAS PREPARED A PLACE FOR YOU IN HEAVEN.

www.PrayerPups.com

PRAYER PUPS BY JEFFREY SMITH

I HAVE TO USE THE CHURCH'S COMPUTER BECAUSE MINE IS ON THE GRITS.

ON THE GRITS? DON'T YOU MEAN "ON THE FRITZ?"

NO. YESTERDAY IT WAS "ON THE FRITZ."

SO TODAY IT'S IN A DUMPSTER OUT BACK OF THE WAFFLE HOUSE.

IF YOU NEED A COMUTER, BUT DON'T HAVE ONE, SEE IF YOUR CHURCH OFFERS THEM IN THE LIBRARY.

www.PrayerPups.com

PRAYER PUPS BY JEFFREY SMITH

PAUL COMPARED THE LIFE OF A CHRISTIAN TO A RACE.

THE LONGER WE RUN, THE HARDER IT IS.

WE GROW TIRED & CARELESS, BUT JESUS WILL HELP EACH OF US WIN OUR RACE.

WHAT KIND OF SHOES DO I NEED TO BUY FOR THIS RACE?

THE RACE PAUL TALKS ABOUT REPRESENTS OUR DAILY BATTLE AGAINST SIN.

www.PrayerPups.com

BE CAREFUL THAT YOUR JOKES DON'T HURT SOMEONE'S FEELINGS.

www.PrayerPups.com

SOMETIMES TALKING ABOUT YOUR FEARS CAN HELP YOU DEAL WITH THEM.

www.PrayerPups.com

WITH GOD, WE HAVE NOTHING TO FEAR.

www.PrayerPups.com

PRAYER PUPS BY JEFFREY SMITH

FOCUSING ON SOMETHING POSITIVE CAN HELP YOU THROUGH A DIFFICULT TIME.

www.PrayerPups.com

PRAYER PUPS BY JEFFREY SMITH

YOUR CHURCH LEADERS CAN HELP YOU REDUCE YOUR FEARS.

www.PrayerPups.com

PRAYER PUPS BY JEFFREY SMITH

PLANT THE SEED OF FAITH IN YOUR SOUL AND WATCH IT GROW.

www.PrayerPups.com

PRAYER PUPS BY JEFFREY SMITH

Panel 1: THE VET MADE MY MASTER PUT ME ON A DIET. / HOW'S THAT GOING?

Panel 2: I REALIZED THAT BEING ON A DIET IS A LOT LIKE OUR JOURNEY AS CHRISTIANS. EVERY MORNING, WE HAVE TO WAKE UP AND MAKE A DECISION TO BE FAITHFUL OR NOT.

Panel 3: YEAH, BUT AT LEAST WITH A DIET, YOU DON'T HAVE THE DEVIL WHISPERING IN YOUR EAR TO BE BAD.

Panel 4: I DON'T KNOW. I'VE ALWAYS THOUGHT THE DEVIL MIGHT COME DRESSED AS A CUPCAKE.

JUST LIKE IN DIETING, WE MUST REMAIN RESOLUTE IN OUR CHRISTIAN WALK.

PRAYER PUPS BY JEFFREY SMITH

Panel 1: THIS DIET HAS ME THINKING ABOUT THE FORBIDDEN FRUIT.

Panel 2: WOW! THAT'S A GREAT WAY TO RELATE YOUR EXPERIENCE TO THE BIBLE, AMOS. YOU KNOW, NO ONE KNOWS WHAT FRUIT IT REALLY WAS. THE IDEA OF IT BEING AN APPLE IS JUST LEGEND. SOME SCHOLARS EVEN SAY IT'S A FRUIT THAT NO LONGER EXISTS.

Panel 3: WHAT KIND OF FRUIT DO YOU THINK IT MIGHT HAVE BEEN?

Panel 4: I'LL BET IT WAS CHOCOLATE FRUIT.

WHAT KIND OF FRUIT DO <u>YOU</u> THINK THE FORBIDDEN FRUIT MIGHT HAVE BEEN?

PRAYER PUPS BY JEFFREY SMITH

Panel 1: WHY DID GOD MAKE ALL THE TASTY FOOD FATTENING & ALL THE HEALTHY FOOD YUCHY?

Panel 2: IT'S NOT YUCHY. YOU JUST HAVE TO TRAIN YOUR PALATE TO ENJOY HEALTHIER FOODS.

Panel 3: TRAIN MY PALATE?!

Panel 4: AND EXACTLY <u>WHERE</u> WILL THEY PUT THE CHOKE COLLAR TO DO THAT?

KEEP YOUR BODY HEALTHY TO SHOW YOUR GRATITUDE TO GOD FOR GIVING IT TO YOU.

PRAYER PUPS BY JEFFREY SMITH

IF ONLY THAT WERE TRUE.

www.PrayerPups.com

PRAYER PUPS BY JEFFREY SMITH

DON'T BELIEVE EVERYTHING YOU HEAR.

www.PrayerPups.com

PRAYER PUPS BY JEFFREY SMITH

MATTHEW 13 TELLS US THE GREATEST REWARDS ARE WORTH THE GREATEST SACRIFICES.

www.PrayerPups.com

PRAYER PUPS BY JEFFREY SMITH

THE STORY OF SAMSON AND DELILAH IS IN JUDGES 16.

PRAYER PUPS BY JEFFREY SMITH

NO ONE KNOWS THE NAME OF NOAH'S WIFE BECAUSE IT'S NEVER MENTIONED IN THE BIBLE.

PRAYER PUPS BY JEFFREY SMITH

LOOK AT WHAT YOU DO TO EXCESS AND ASK, "IS THIS INTERFERING WITH MY RELATIONSHIP WITH GOD?"

PRAYER PUPS BY JEFFREY SMITH

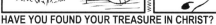

WHAT'S UP, AMOS? WHY AREN'T YOU DRESSED FOR EXPLORING?

WE SAID WE WERE GOING TO LOOK FOR HIDDEN TREASURE.

I KNOW.

BUT I GAVE IT A LOT OF THOUGHT AND I REALIZED SOMETHING.

I'VE ALREADY FOUND MY TREASURE!

HAVE YOU FOUND YOUR TREASURE IN CHRIST?

PRAYER PUPS BY JEFFREY SMITH

PROFESSOR AMOS, MY MASTER AND I ARE FIGHTING LATELY.

SOUNDS LIKE THE TWO OF YOU NEED A GOOD OBEDIENCE CLASS.

I DON'T THINK SO. WE TRIED THAT LAST YEAR...

AND HE WAS NO MORE OBEDIENT COMING OUT AS HE WAS GOING IN!

MANY OF US NEED AN "OBEDIENCE TO GOD" CLASS!

PRAYER PUPS BY JEFFREY SMITH

HAVE YOU BEEN GOING TO THE DIET CLASSES AT CHURCH?

YEP, FOR ABOUT A WEEK.

WELL, I CAN TELL IT'S WORKING.

REALLY??!!!

I MUST LOOK FANTASTIC!!! I KNEW THE DIET WAS WORKING, BUT I HAD NO IDEA YOU'D SEE SUCH A BIG DIFFERENCE IN SO SHORT A TIME. LOOK AT YOU, YOU CAN'T KEEP YOUR EYES OFF ME! I MUST REALLY BE FABULOUS!

A LITTLE COMPLIMENT GOES A LONG WAY WITH NIM.

WHO'S GOT A CAMERA? SOMEONE NEEDS TO GET A PICTURE OF ME...QUICK!

A SMALL COMPLIMENT TO SOMEONE YOU LOVE CAN GO A LONG WAY.

PRAYER PUPS BY JEFFREY SMITH

JESUS FED THE MULTITUDE WITH 5 LOAVES AND 2 FISHES.

www.PrayerPups.com

PRAYER PUPS BY JEFFREY SMITH

"IN HIS HAND IS THE LIFE OF EVERY CREATURE AND THE BREATH OF ALL MANKIND." - JOB 12:10

www.PrayerPups.com

PRAYER PUPS BY JEFFREY SMITH

VACATION IS A GREAT TIME TO VISIT A CHURCH IN A NEW TOWN.

www.PrayerPups.com

PRAYER PUPS BY JEFFREY SMITH

JESUS SAID, "I AM THE ALPHA AND THE OMEGA, THE FIRST AND LAST, THE BEGINNING AND THE END." www.PrayerPups.com

PRAYER PUPS BY JEFFREY SMITH

EVERYONE HAS A FAVORITE TRANSLATION OF THE BIBLE, AND GOD USES EACH OF THEM FOR HIS GLORY. www.PrayerPups.com

PRAYER PUPS BY JEFFREY SMITH

LIVE YOUR LIFE AS A TESTAMENT TO GOD'S LOVING GRACE. www.PrayerPups.com

PRAYER PUPS BY JEFFREY SMITH

NIM! BUDDY! LOOK AT YOU! YOU'VE LOST ALL YOUR EXTRA WEIGHT!

THAT CHURCH DIET PLAN REALLY DID THE JOB!

I KNOW! I LOST 75 POUNDS!

75 POUNDS? THAT SOUNDS LIKE A WHOPPER.

NOPE. WHOPPERS AREN'T ALLOWED ON THIS DIET.

YOUR CHURCH PROBABLY HAS A LOT OF PROGRAMS TO HELP YOU REACH YOUR GOALS.

www.PrayerPups.com

PRAYER PUPS BY JEFFREY SMITH

"SOMETIMES I LIKE TO SING GOD'S PRAISES WITH ALL MY FRIENDS AT A CONCERT."

"SOMETIMES I LIKE TO STUDY THE WORD OF GOD IN A SMALL GROUP SETTING."

"BUT SOMETIMES I JUST LIKE TO SPEND QUALITY TIME ALONE WITH GOD. JUST ME AND HIM."

"THAT'S THE TIME I LIKE BEST OF ALL!"

JESUS MADE TIME TO SPEND ALONE WITH GOD. YOU SHOULD DO THE SAME.

www.PrayerPups.com

PRAYER PUPS BY JEFFREY SMITH

SOME GUY'S TRYING TO SELL BLESSINGS ON EBAY.

THAT'S SILLY!

EVERYBODY KNOWS AMAZON IS THE BEST PLACE TO ORDER BLESSINGS.

THE SHIPPING CHARGES ARE MORE PREDICTABLE.

BLESSINGS CAN'T BE BOUGHT OR SOLD, THEY'RE ONLY AVAILABLE THROUGH THE GRACE OF GOD.

www.PrayerPups.com

PRAYER PUPS BY JEFFREY SMITH

A PODCAST IS A GREAT WAY TO BROADCAST YOUR CHURCH'S MESSAGE TO MORE PEOPLE.

www.PrayerPups.com

PRAYER PUPS BY JEFFREY SMITH

NO ONE KNOWS WHAT TYPE OF FRUIT GREW ON THE TREE OF KNOWLEDGE.

www.PrayerPups.com

PRAYER PUPS BY JEFFREY SMITH

THERE ARE A LOT OF ORGANIZATIONS YOU MAY HAVE NEVER HEARD OF THAT DO THE WORK OF CHRIST.

www.PrayerPups.com

PRAYER PUPS BY JEFFREY SMITH

THE FATHER SAID TO HIS SERVANTS, "QUICK! BRING THE BEST ROBE AND PUT IT ON HIM! PUT A RING ON HIS FINGER AND SANDALS ON HIS FEET."

"BRING THE FATTENED CALF AND KILL IT. LET'S HAVE A FEAST AND CELEBRATE. FOR THIS SON OF MINE WAS DEAD AND IS ALIVE AGAIN; HE WAS LOST AND IS FOUND."

AND THEY ALL CELEBRATED!

WELL, EXCEPT FOR THE COW.

YOU CAN READ ABOUT THE PRODIGAL SON IN THE GOSPEL OF LUKE.

www.PrayerPups.com

PRAYER PUPS BY JEFFREY SMITH

PUGS ARE CHINESE, RIGHT?

THEN WHY DON'T YOU DO SOMETHING ABOUT THE FACT THAT THE CHINESE AREN'T ALLOWED TO PRAY OR EVEN OWN A BIBLE?

I HAVE BEEN DOING SOMETHING ABOUT IT.

WHAT?

PRAYING FOR THEM!

WE SHOULD ALL PRAY FOR OUR BROTHERS AND SISTERS IN CHRIST WHO ARE PERSECUTED.

www.PrayerPups.com

PRAYER PUPS BY JEFFREY SMITH

I KNOW SOMEBODY WHO ALWAYS COMPLAINS. SHE NEVER SEES THE BLESSINGS IN HER LIFE.

YOU SHOULD PRAY FOR HER. PRAY THAT GOD WILL REVEAL HER BLESSINGS AND THEN TOUCH HER HEART SO THAT SHE CAN FOCUS ON THE POSITIVE. WHICH WILL HELP HER DEAL WITH HER DIFFICULTIES MORE EASILY.

I WAS JUST GOING TO TELL HER TO SHUT HER KIBBLE-HOLE AND QUIT COMPLAINING, BUT YOUR WAY SOUNDS BETTER.

IF YOU REMEMBER YOUR BLESSINGS, IT'S EASIER TO DEAL WITH YOUR PROBLEMS.

www.PrayerPups.com

PRAYER PUPS BY JEFFREY SMITH

YOU LIED TO ME! YOU SAID PRAYER WORKS, BUT IT DOESN'T!

WHAT?

I PRAYED FOR A MILLION DOLLARS AND I DIDN'T GET SQUAT.

THAT'S NOT PRAYER! THAT'S JUST LOOKING TO GOD TO JUST GIVE YOU WHAT YOU WANT. HONEST PRAYER IS SELFLESS AND SINCERE. IT DRAWS YOU CLOSER TO GOD.

I GUESS I NEED TO CALL THE DEALERSHIP AND CANCEL MY PORSCHE, HUH?

A PORSCHE? WHAT WOULD YOU DO WITH A PORSCHE?

GIVE IT TO MY OWNER SO I COULD HANG MY HEAD OUT THE WINDOW LIKE THIS!

KEEP YOUR PRAYER SINCERE AND GOD-CENTERED.

www.PrayerPups.com

PRAYER PUPS BY JEFFREY SMITH

I'VE STARTED WRITING FOR THE CHURCH NEWSLETTER.

THAT'S GREAT!

YEAH, AND I'M NOT GOING TO JUST WRITE FLUFF-PIECES EITHER. I'M GOING TO BE A HARD-HITTING, TAKE-NO-PRISONERS, INVESTIGATIVE JOURNALIST.

I'M GOING TO USE THE TIME-HONORED TOOLS OF BASELESS ACCUSATIONS, INNUENDO AND FEAR TO WHIP MY READERS INTO A FURY! NOW I JUST NEED A JUICY SUBJECT FOR MY FIRST PULITZER PRIZE-WINNING STORY!

I DON'T KNOW IF...

I'VE GOT IT! WEDNESDAY NIGHT SUPPERS: WHAT ARE YOU REALLY EATING?!!!

IF YOU'RE A GOOD WRITER, WHY NOT CONTRIBUTE TO YOUR CHURCH'S BULLETIN OR WEBSITE?

www.PrayerPups.com

PRAYER PUPS BY JEFFREY SMITH

SO, I HEAR YOU'RE WRITING FOR THE CHURCH BULLETIN.

YEP!

I'VE FOUND MY TRUE CALLING. I'M GOING TO RIP THE LID OFF CORRUPTION, TAKE ON THE SPECIAL INTERESTS AND INVOKE FEAR AT THE VERY MENTION OF MY NAME.

MMM HMM. AND WHAT DID YOU WRITE ABOUT THE CHURCH PICNIC?

PISH, POSH! NOBODY CARES ABOUT THAT TRIFFLE.

I CARE!

NO, YOU JUST THINK YOU DO. MY JOB IS TO TELL YOU WHAT YOU SHOULD CARE ABOUT.

YOUR BULLETIN IS FULL OF INTERESTING THINGS HAPPENING AROUND YOUR CHURCH.

www.PrayerPups.com

PRAYER PUPS BY JEFFREY SMITH

BEING SKEPTICAL IS A GOOD IDEA IN MANY SITUATIONS, BUT DON'T BECOME CYNICAL TOWARD GOD.   www.PrayerPups.com

PRAYER PUPS BY JEFFREY SMITH

YOUR CHURCH'S BULLETIN SHOULD KEEP THE WHOLE CONGREGATION IN THE LOOP.   www.PrayerPups.com

PRAYER PUPS BY JEFFREY SMITH

SOME CHURCHES ARE BIG...SOME ARE SMALL. WHAT'S IMPORTANT IS THAT THEY DO THE WORK OF GOD.   www.PrayerPups.com

PRAYER PUPS BY JEFFREY SMITH

I'M SINGING A SOLO IN CHURCH ON SUNDAY MORNING.

THAT'S GREAT, AMOS! I LOVE IT WHEN YOU SING. AND APPARENTLY EVERYONE ELSE DOES TOO, SINCE YOU GET LOTS OF APPLAUSE.

IT MUST FEEL GOOD TO HAVE PEOPLE APPLAUD YOU.

YEAH, BUT IT FEELS BETTER KNOWING THEY'RE REALLY APPLAUDING GOD.

NEVER FORGET THAT WHATEVER TALENT YOU HAVE IS REALLY A GIFT FROM GOD.

www.PrayerPups.com

PRAYER PUPS BY JEFFREY SMITH

I HAVE A QUESTION.   SHOOT.

I HEAR THAT IN HEAVEN, THE STREETS ARE PAVED IN GOLD.

THAT'S RIGHT. REVELATION 21 TELLS OF A NEW HEAVEN AND A NEW EARTH WITH A GREAT STREET MADE OF GOLD.

THEN ARE THE OLYMPIC MEDALS MADE OF ASPHALT?

REVELATION 21 DESCRIBES THE ARCHITECTURE OF THE AFTERLIFE.

www.PrayerPups.com

PRAYER PUPS BY JEFFREY SMITH

MY PASTOR SAID GOD IS LOVE.   THAT'S RIGHT.

BUT THE WORD LOVE IS VERB, LIKE IN "I LOVE TO DANCE." SAYING SOMEONE IS A VERB DOESN'T MAKE SENSE. MAYBE I SHOULD START SAYING, "ABBY IS DANCE."

LOVE CAN ALSO BE A NOUN, LIKE IN "HE HAS A LOT OF LOVE." IT'S USED LIKE THAT.

OH.

CAN I STILL SAY "ABBY IS DANCE?"

GOD IS LOVE.

www.PrayerPups.com

PRAYER PUPS BY JEFFREY SMITH

THE CHURCH'S DIET PLAN EVEN LETS ME HAVE PEANUT BUTTER.

YOU KNOW, 2 TABLESPOONS OF PEANUT BUTTER HAS VITAMINS E & B6, MAGNESIUM & POTASSIUM. IT CAN REDUCE YOUR RISK OF HEART DISEASE AND LOWERS THE RISK OF DIABETES BY 30 PERCENT.

WOW!

I ATE A WHOLE JAR THIS MORNING...IMAGINE HOW HEALTHY I AM!

REMEMBER TO HAVE MODERATION IN ALL THINGS...EXCEPT IN YOUR LOVE OF GOD.

PRAYER PUPS BY JEFFREY SMITH

SINCE PEANUTS ARE ON THE DIET, I ATE A WHOLE BAG!

THAT'S NOT BEING ON THE DIET, AMOS. YOU'RE ONLY SUPPOSED TO EAT ONE SERVING, NOT A WHOLE BAG. THE CHURCH DIET PLAN IS VERY CLEAR ON THE RULES.

OOPS! I DIDN'T REALIZE THEY WERE RULES.

WHAT DID YOU THINK THEY WERE?

I DON'T KNOW. SUGGESTIONS?

DON'T VIEW GOD'S RULES AS "SUGGESTIONS."

PRAYER PUPS BY JEFFREY SMITH

OUR CHURCH HAD A BIG ICE CREAM SOCIAL LAST NIGHT.

DIDN'T THAT MESS UP YOUR DIET?

NOPE, I TOOK SOME ALL-NATURAL, NO-SUGAR, NO-FAT, HI-FIBER, NON-DAIRY FROZEN DESSERT FOOD.

WHAT FLAVOR?

THE PACKAGE SAID "BANANA SPLIT BLAST," BUT IT TASTED MORE LIKE "FEET BLAST."

IF YOUR CHURCH HASN'T HAD AN ICE CREAM SOCIAL, GET ONE STARTED!

PRAYER PUPS BY JEFFREY SMITH

DIET CLASSES TIED TO CHURCH GROUPS OFFER A BETTER CHANCE AT WEIGHT LOSS SUCCESS.

www.PrayerPups.com

PRAYER PUPS BY JEFFREY SMITH

BE NICE TO YOUR ENEMIES, IT MIGHT HELP BRING THEM TO JESUS.

www.PrayerPups.com

PRAYER PUPS BY JEFFREY SMITH

NO MATTER HOW YOU EXPRESS IT, THE MESSAGE IS THE SAME: GOOD WILL TRIUMPH OVER EVIL.

www.PrayerPups.com

PRAYER PUPS BY JEFFREY SMITH

DON'T GIVE IN TO EVIL BY DOING EVIL YOURSELF.

PRAYER PUPS BY JEFFREY SMITH

YOUR RELATIONSHIP WITH GOD IS WHAT IS MOST IMPORTANT, NOT YOUR OWN DESIRES.

PRAYER PUPS BY JEFFREY SMITH

WHEN THE BIBLE SPEAKS OF ALIENS, IT MEANS PEOPLE FROM OTHER COUNTRIES.

PRAYER PUPS BY JEFFREY SMITH

THE BIBLE SAYS WE SHOULD CARE FOR THE ALIENS, BUT IT MEANS PEOPLE FROM FOREIGN COUNTRIES.   www.PrayerPups.com

PRAYER PUPS BY JEFFREY SMITH

THE BIBLE: THE TRUTH IS IN THERE.   www.PrayerPups.com

PRAYER PUPS BY JEFFREY SMITH

THE LORD IS COMPASSIONATE AND GRACIOUS, SLOW TO ANGER, ABOUNDING IN LOVE. HE WILL NOT ALWAYS ACCUSE, NOR WILL HE HARBOR HIS ANGER FOREVER;

HE DOES NOT TREAT US AS OUR SINS DESERVE OR REPAY US ACCORDING TO OUR INIQUITIES. FOR AS HIGH AS THE HEAVENS ARE ABOVE THE EARTH, SO GREAT IS HIS LOVE FOR THOSE WHO FEAR HIM;

AS FAR AS THE EAST IS FROM THE WEST, SO FAR HAS HE REMOVED OUR TRANSGRESSIONS FROM US. AS A FATHER HAS COMPASSION ON HIS CHILDREN, SO THE LORD HAS COMPASSION ON THOSE WHO FEAR HIM.
- PSALM 103:8-13

GOD DOESN'T LOVE US FOR BECAUSE OF OUR ACTIONS. HE LOVES US IN SPITE OF OUR ACTIONS!

WE COULD NEVER BE GOOD ENOUGH FOR GOD. THAT'S WHY JESUS SAVED US.   www.PrayerPups.com

PRAYER PUPS BY JEFFREY SMITH

WELL, IT TOOK EVERY PENNY I HAD, BUT NOW I'M PREPARED!

I DIDN'T WANT TO BE WITHOUT LAMP OIL LIKE THE VIRGINS IN MATTHEW 25, SO I BOUGHT 40 CASES OF THE STUFF!

ABBY, SURELY YOU KNOW THAT THE PARABLE OF TEN VIRGINS IS A METAPHOR FOR THE FACT THAT WE ALL NEED TO BE SPIRITUALLY PREPARED FOR CHRIST'S RETURN. NOT THAT WE NEED TO BUY LAMP OIL!

SO I SPENT ALL THIS MONEY ON OIL WHEN I COULD HAVE SPENT IT ON NEW SHOES?!

NONE OF US KNOWS THE HOUR OF JESUS' RETURN, SO WE MUST BE READY AT ALL TIMES.

PRAYER PUPS BY JEFFREY SMITH

EVERYONE ELSE IS TALLER THAN ME AND I'M SICK OF IT!

IT DOESN'T MATTER HOW TALL YOU ARE, NIM. WHAT MATTERS IS THAT YOU'RE GROWING IN YOUR FAITH.

THE ONLY WAY WE CAN HELP OTHERS AND DO GOD'S WORK IS IF WE'RE "SPIRITUALLY"-TALL.

WHERE CAN I FIND A RULER TO MEASURE THAT?

MAKE SURE YOU GROW IN YOUR FAITH AS YOU GROW OLDER. DON'T ALLOW YOURSELF TO BECOME A SPIRITUAL "PIP-SQUEAK."

PRAYER PUPS BY JEFFREY SMITH

JESUS LOVES THE LITTLE CHILDREN, ALL THE CHILDREN OF THE WORLD!

RED AND YELLOW, BLACK AND WHITE, THEY ARE PRECIOUS IN HIS SIGHT!

JESUS LOVES THE LITTLE CHILDREN OF THE WOOOOOORLD!!!

I DIDN'T SEE "FURRY" IN THAT LIST.

JESUS LOVES ALL OF US, NO MATTER WHO WE ARE.

PRAYER PUPS BY JEFFREY SMITH

PROFESSOR AMOS, WHAT'S THE SECRET TO A HAPPY LIFE?

A STRONG LOVE OF GOD.

THAT'S SO TRUE.

AND A CUPCAKE EVERY ONCE IN A WHILE DOESN'T HURT.

LOVE GOD WITH ALL YOUR HEART AND HE WILL REWARD YOU WITH TRUE JOY.

www.PrayerPups.com

PRAYER PUPS BY JEFFREY SMITH

DID YOU KNOW THAT DAVID WAS IN A BAND?

REALLY?

YEAH!

AND HE REALLY "ROCKED" GOLIATH'S WORLD!

I KEEP WALKING INTO 'EM

HEEHEEHEEHEE!

DAVID WASN'T AFRAID OF GOLIATH BECAUSE HE KNEW HE HAD GOD ON HIS SIDE.

www.PrayerPups.com

PRAYER PUPS BY JEFFREY SMITH

KNOCK! KNOCK!

WHO'S THERE?

MESHACK, SHADRACK

MESHACK, SHADRACK WHO?

MESHACK, SHADRACK AND ABEDNEGOOOOOOOOOOOOOOO!!!

THANKS, ZANE! THIS GAG WOULDN'T HAVE WORKED WITHOUT YOUR HELP.

www.PrayerPups.com

PRAYER PUPS BY JEFFREY SMITH

HAVE YOU FIGURED OUT WHAT SPECIAL TALENT GOD GAVE YOU TO USE FOR HIS PURPOSE?

I TRIED, BUT I'M GOOD AT EVERYTHING!

NIM, YOU NEED TO BE MORE HUMBLE.

MORE HUMBLE?

BUT HUMILITY IS MY BEST QUALITY.

WHOEVER EXALTS HIMSELF WILL BE HUMBLED, AND HE WHO HUMBLES HIMSELF WILL BE EXALTED.

www.PrayerPups.com

PRAYER PUPS BY JEFFREY SMITH

TODAY IN SUNDAY SCHOOL, WE LEARNED ABOUT JESUS AND THE THREE WISE GUYS.

YOU MEAN "THREE WISE MEN."

THAT DOES MAKE A LITTLE MORE SENSE.

IF YOU DON'T UNDERSTAND SOMETHING IN THE BIBLE, ASK SOMEONE WHO DOES TO EXPLAIN IT TO YOU.

www.PrayerPups.com

PRAYER PUPS BY JEFFREY SMITH

SO THE MORAL OF PAUL AND THE RIOT IN EPHESUS...

...IS THAT WE SHOULD NEVER BLINDLY FOLLOW THE CROWD.

OH, I NEVER BLINDLY FOLLOW THE CROWD.

AND YOU DON'T THINK I SHOULD. RIGHT?

PAUL TOLD THE EPHESIANS ABOUT JESUS, EVEN THOUGH THEY TRIED TO SILENCE HIM.

www.PrayerPups.com

PRAYER PUPS BY JEFFREY SMITH

IT'S OKAY IF YOU DON'T "DRESS UP" FOR CHURCH. BUT DON'T "DRESS DOWN" FOR IT, EITHER.

www.PrayerPups.com

PRAYER PUPS BY JEFFREY SMITH

TITHING TO YOUR CHURCH EACH WEEK IS VERY IMPORTANT.

www.PrayerPups.com

PRAYER PUPS BY JEFFREY SMITH

THE HOLY SPIRIT LIVES INSIDE EVERYONE WHO TRUSTS IN JESUS AS HIS OR HER SAVIOR.

www.PrayerPups.com

PRAYER PUPS BY JEFFREY SMITH

THE LAND OF MILK AND HONEY WAS THE HOME THAT GOD PROMISED TO HIS CHOSEN PEOPLE.

www.PrayerPups.com

PRAYER PUPS BY JEFFREY SMITH

DON'T BE ANGRY AT THOSE WHO DON'T KNOW GOD, PRAY FOR THEM TO SEE THE TRUTH!

www.PrayerPups.com

PRAYER PUPS BY JEFFREY SMITH

THE BIBLE CAN HELP US UNDERSTAND WHAT'S REAL AND WHAT'S MAKE BELIEVE.

www.PrayerPups.com

PRAYER PUPS BY JEFFREY SMITH

WHEN YOU LOVE GOD, YOU JUST CAN'T HIDE IT.

www.PrayerPups.com

PRAYER PUPS BY JEFFREY SMITH

CHURCH SUPPERS ARE GREAT WAYS TO ENJOY FELLOWSHIP.

www.PrayerPups.com

PRAYER PUPS BY JEFFREY SMITH

YOU CAN DO ALL THINGS THROUGH GOD WHO STRENGTHENS YOU!

www.PrayerPups.com

PRAYER PUPS BY JEFFREY SMITH

CLAP! | WHY ARE YOU CLAPPING YOUR HANDS? | IT SAYS IN PSALM 47 TO "CLAP YOUR HANDS"... CLAP! CLAP! | AND "SHOUT TO GOD WITH A JUBILANT CRY!" CLAP! CLAP! AAAAWWHHOOOO!!! | WHAT YOU LACK IN RHYTHM, YOU MAKE UP FOR IN ENTHUSIASM. CLAP!

DON'T BE AFRAID TO SHOW HOW MUCH YOU LOVE GOD...NO MATTER WHAT ANYBODY ELSE THINKS!   www.**PrayerPups**.com

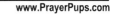

PRAYER PUPS BY JEFFREY SMITH

DOES GOD LOVE CATS? | SURE. GOD LOVES ALL OF US. | REALLY?!!! EVEN CATS?!!! | I'M AFRAID SO. | I GUESS THERE'S STILL A LOT I NEED TO LEARN ABOUT GOD. | AMEN TO THAT, BROTHER!

JESUS SAID TO LOVE EVERYONE...EVEN YOUR ENEMIES. IF SOMEONE DOES YOU WRONG, PRAY FOR THEM.   www.PrayerPups.com

PRAYER PUPS BY JEFFREY SMITH

LICK LICK LICK LICK | LICK LICK LICK LICK | LICK LICK LICK LICK | I LOVE PEANUT BUTTER. MMM, HMM.

EVERYTHING THAT YOU LOVE COMES FROM GOD.   www.**PrayerPups**.com

PRAYER PUPS BY JEFFREY SMITH

REMEMBER TO TAKE TIME FOR GOD WHEN SCHOOL STARTS AND YOU GET BUSY.

www.PrayerPups.com

PRAYER PUPS BY JEFFREY SMITH

GOD WILL PROTECT YOU FROM TROUBLE.

www.PrayerPups.com

PRAYER PUPS BY JEFFREY SMITH

DON'T BE SAD FOR WHAT'S ENDING. BE THANKFUL YOU WERE ABLE TO EXPERIENCE IT.

www.PrayerPups.com

PRAYER PUPS BY JEFFREY SMITH

GOD WILL PROTECT YOU FROM EVIL.

www.PrayerPups.com

PRAYER PUPS BY JEFFREY SMITH

MAKE SURE THE ENTERTAINMENT YOU WATCH DOESN'T WORK AGAINST GOD'S LAWS.

www.PrayerPups.com

PRAYER PUPS BY JEFFREY SMITH

REMEMBER THAT GOD WANTS US TO SHARE WHAT WE HAVE WITH OTHERS.

www.PrayerPups.com

PRAYER PUPS BY JEFFREY SMITH

MAKE SURE TO LISTEN WHEN GOD CALLS YOU TO DO SOMETHING.

PRAYER PUPS BY JEFFREY SMITH

HAPPY BIRTHDAY, MOM!

PRAYER PUPS BY JEFFREY SMITH

BE PATIENT. GOD WILL REVEAL HIS PLAN FOR YOUR LIFE IN HIS OWN TIME.

PRAYER PUPS BY JEFFREY SMITH

BE CAREFUL NOT TO DO THE THINGS YOU WANT INSTEAD OF WHAT GOD WANTS YOU TO DO.

www.PrayerPups.com

PRAYER PUPS BY JEFFREY SMITH

SOMETIMES WE DON'T NOTICE HOW GOD HAS BLESSED US.

www.PrayerPups.com

PRAYER PUPS BY JEFFREY SMITH

BE CAREFUL THAT THE DESIRES OF YOUR HEART DON'T INTERFERE WITH YOUR WALK WITH GOD.

www.PrayerPups.com

PRAYER PUPS BY JEFFREY SMITH

OKAY, NIM. IT'S TIME FOR YOU TO DROP THIS "GREATNESS" THING.

BUT I'M GREAT AT BEING GREAT!

NO, YOU'RE GREAT AT BEING SELF-IMPORTANT. YOU DON'T WANT TO BE GREAT FOR THE RIGHT REASONS.

GREAT AT BEING SELF-IMPORTANT, HUH? SO THE KEY POINT HERE IS THAT YOU THINK I AM GREAT AT SOMETHING, RIGHT?

ARE YOU EVEN LISTENING TO ME?

WHAT?

THOSE WHO LOVE US CAN HELP US STAY ON THE RIGHT PATH TO GOD.

www.PrayerPups.com

PRAYER PUPS BY JEFFREY SMITH

IF GOD HAS GREATNESS PLANNED FOR YOU, YOU'LL HAVE IT.

BUT IF YOU TRY TO FORCE IT, YOU'LL END UP MISSING THE BLESSINGS OF GREATNESS HE HAS IN MIND FOR YOU.

SO WHAT I HEAR YOU SAY IS THAT I'LL BE GREAT IN THE FUTURE.

I THINK YOU'RE RIGHT. I CAN FEEL THE FUTURE GREATNESS BUBBLING UP INSIDE ME.

IT'S PROBABLY JUST HOT AIR.

PROVERBS SAYS THAT PRIDE GOES BEFORE A FALL.

www.PrayerPups.com

PRAYER PUPS BY JEFFREY SMITH

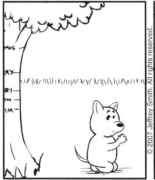

GOD, EVERYONE THINKS I'M BEING SELF-ABSORBED.

IF YOU DISAGREE WITH THEM, PLEASE SEND ME A SIGN.

OOPS.

PRAYER WILL HELP YOU TO KNOW GOD'S WILL FOR YOUR LIFE.

www.PrayerPups.com

PRAYER PUPS BY JEFFREY SMITH

MAKE SURE YOUR OWN HOUSE IS IN ORDER BEFORE GIVING ADVICE TO OTHERS.

PRAYER PUPS BY JEFFREY SMITH

WHEN YOU DO SOMETHING BAD, ASK GOD FOR FORGIVENESS RIGHT AWAY.

PRAYER PUPS BY JEFFREY SMITH

IT'S OKAY TO READ COMIC BOOKS, BUT MAKE TIME TO READ THE BIBLE, TOO.

PRAYER PUPS BY JEFFREY SMITH

MANNA WAS A FREE GIFT FROM GOD...IT COULDN'T BE BOUGHT. JUST LIKE CHRIST'S SALVATION.

www.PrayerPups.com

PRAYER PUPS BY JEFFREY SMITH

GOD MADE THE WORLD IN SEVEN DAYS. READ ABOUT IT IN GENESIS 1 & 2.

www.PrayerPups.com

PRAYER PUPS BY JEFFREY SMITH

GOD KNOWS WHAT YOU REALLY WANT.

www.PrayerPups.com

PRAYER PUPS BY JEFFREY SMITH

GROW WHERE YOU ARE PLANTED.

www.PrayerPups.com

PRAYER PUPS BY JEFFREY SMITH

WE SHOULD ALL TRY TO BE MORE LIKE JESUS. BUT MAKE SURE OF WHAT YOU'RE DOING!

www.PrayerPups.com

PRAYER PUPS BY JEFFREY SMITH

GOD KNEW YOU BEFORE YOU WERE BORN. HE'S LOVED YOU LONGER THAN YOU'VE BEEN ALIVE.

www.PrayerPups.com

PRAYER PUPS BY JEFFREY SMITH

"SURELY GOODNESS AND MERCY SHALL FOLLOW ME ALL THE DAYS OF MY LIFE."

www.PrayerPups.com

PRAYER PUPS BY JEFFREY SMITH

LET THE LORD BE YOUR SHEPHERD. LET HIM GUIDE YOU TO THE LIFE HE HAS PLANNED FOR YOU.

www.PrayerPups.com

PRAYER PUPS BY JEFFREY SMITH

JESUS PERFORMED MANY MIRACLES, BUT NIM DIDN'T GET ANY OF THEM RIGHT!

www.PrayerPups.com

PRAYER PUPS BY JEFFREY SMITH

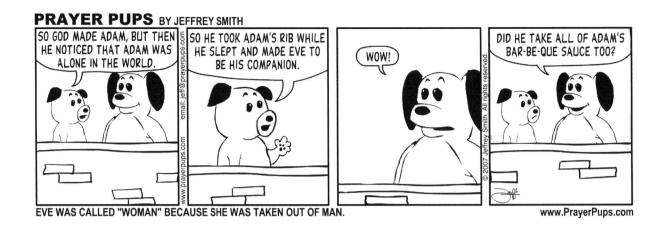

EVE WAS CALLED "WOMAN" BECAUSE SHE WAS TAKEN OUT OF MAN.   www.PrayerPups.com

PRAYER PUPS BY JEFFREY SMITH

VISITING THE CHURCHES OF FAMILY MEMBERS IS A GOOD WAY TO LEARN HOW OTHERS WORSHIP JESUS.   www.PrayerPups.com

PRAYER PUPS BY JEFFREY SMITH

THE FEAR OF THE LORD IS THE BEGINNING OF KNOWLEDGE. - PROVERBS 1:7   www.PrayerPups.com

PRAYER PUPS BY JEFFREY SMITH

BURNT OFFERINGS WERE SACRED SACRIFICES TO GOD PEOPLE USED BEFORE JESUS DIED FOR OUR SINS.   www.PrayerPups.com

PRAYER PUPS BY JEFFREY SMITH

MATTHEW 1:1 SHOWS THE GENEALOGY OF JESUS. IT'S HARD TO REMEMBER, BUT IT'S IMPORTANT.   www.PrayerPups.com

PRAYER PUPS BY JEFFREY SMITH

WHEN YOU GO TO CHURCH AND PRAISE GOD IN WORD AND SONG, IT PLEASES HIM.   www.PrayerPups.com

PRAYER PUPS BY JEFFREY SMITH

Panel 1: DO YOU KNOW WHAT FRANKINCENSE IS?

Panel 2: SURE.

Panel 3: LET ME HEAR YOU USE IT IN A SENTENCE.

Panel 4: MY HOUSE SMELLS LIKE HOT DOGS SINCE I GOT SOME FRANK-INCENSE.

FRANKINCENSE WAS ONE OF THE GIFTS THE THREE WISE MEN BROUGHT TO BABY JESUS.

www.PrayerPups.com

PRAYER PUPS BY JEFFREY SMITH

Panel 1: JESUS FED 5000 PEOPLE...

Panel 2: WITH 5 LOAVES AND 5 FISHES.

Panel 3: HOW ABOUT THAT MIRACLE?

Panel 4: HE SHOULD OPEN A RESTAURANT.

JESUS PERFORMED MANY MIRACLES BUT "THE LOAVES & THE FISHES" IS ONE OF THE MOST WELL-KNOWN.

www.PrayerPups.com

PRAYER PUPS BY JEFFREY SMITH

Panel 1: THE GOLDEN CALF AARON BUILT WAS IDOLATRY.

Panel 2: SO GOD TOLD MOSES TO GET RID OF THE CALF.

Panel 3: AND THAT'S WHERE WE GET THE WORD "DE-CALF."

Panel 4: NO IT'S NOT. / CAN I GET A REFILL HERE?

AARON MELTED DOWN ALL THE GOLD EARRINGS THE ISRAELITES HAD TO BUILD THE GOLDEN CALF.

www.PrayerPups.com

PRAYER PUPS BY JEFFREY SMITH

WHAT A LOVELY ROSE!
IT'S A CHRYSANTHEMUM.

IT'S CALLED THE BIBLE LEAF.
HOW DO YOU SPELL CHRYSANTHEMUM?

C...R...WAIT. C...H...R... UM...K...R...I...

WELL, I'LL BE. THIS IS A ROSE, ISN'T IT?

SINCE THE CHRYSANTHEMUM IS CALLED THE "BIBLE LEAF," MANY CHURCHES HOST CHRYSANTHEMUM TEAS.   www.PrayerPups.com

PRAYER PUPS BY JEFFREY SMITH

CON, DO YOU EVER FEEL SELF-CONSCIOUS?

SURE, ABBY. WE ALL DO SOMETIME.

BUT IF WE REMEMBER THAT GOD CREATED US, IT'S EASY TO BEAT THE BLUES.

BECAUSE GOD DOESN'T MAKE ANY MISTAKES.

GOD CREATED YOU IN HIS IMAGE AND HE LOVES YOU WITH ALL HIS HEART!   www.PrayerPups.com

PRAYER PUPS BY JEFFREY SMITH

MY CHILDREN'S MINISTER ASKED ME WHAT THE EPISTLES WERE.

AND I SAID, "THEY WERE THE WIVES OF THE APOSTLES."

WHAT DID HE SAY?

NOT MUCH. HE JUST PUT HIS FACE IN HIS HANDS AND MUMBLED "GIVE ME STRENGTH, LORD."

THE EPISTLES WERE LETTERS PAUL WROTE THAT ARE NOW BOOKS IN THE BIBLE.   www.PrayerPups.com

PRAYER PUPS BY JEFFREY SMITH

I ASKED MY CHILDREN'S MINISTER ABOUT SUNDAY SCHOOL.

I SAID, "HEY DUDE! WHY IS SUNDAY SCHOOL ON SUNDAY?"

I THOUGHT THAT SUNDAY WAS SUPPOSED TO BE OUR DAY OF REST!

I'VE NEVER SEEN ANYONE'S FACE GET THAT RED BEFORE.

THE SABBATH IS OUR DAY OF REST SO THAT WE CAN FOCUS ON OUR RELATIONSHIP WITH GOD.   www.PrayerPups.com

PRAYER PUPS BY JEFFREY SMITH

WHAT ARE YOU DOING?

TITHING.

ISN'T TITHING GIVING MONEY TO THE CHURCH?

IT CAN BE. BUT TITHING IS REALLY GIVING BACK TO GOD FOR ALL HE GIVES US. I DON'T HAVE MONEY, BUT I CAN PLANT FLOWERS TO SAY THANK YOU.

CAN I PLANT ONE TOO?

TITHING LETS GOD KNOW THAT YOU HAVE GRATITUDE FOR ALL HE GIVES YOU.   www.PrayerPups.com

PRAYER PUPS BY JEFFREY SMITH

YOU MADE A GREAT CHURCH BULLETIN THIS WEEK. BUT YOU MISPELLED "MESSAGES."

THIS SAYS THAT "MASSAGES" MAY BE GIVEN TO THE PASTOR'S SECRETARY.

!

NO WONDER SHE LOOKED SO RELAXED ALL WEEK.

CHURCH BULLETINS ARE FUN TO READ EACH WEEK TO SEE WHAT'S HAPPENING AT THE CHURCH.   www.PrayerPups.com

PRAYER PUPS BY JEFFREY SMITH

YOUR CHURCH OFFERS MANY OPPORTUNITIES FOR INVOLVEMENT. FIND OUT WHERE YOU CAN SHINE!

PRAYER PUPS BY JEFFREY SMITH

LEARNING TO HEAR GOD TAKES TIME, BUT IT'S WORTH THE EFFORT.

PRAYER PUPS BY JEFFREY SMITH

WHEN SOLOMON DEDICATED THE TEMPLE TO THE LORD, THEPEOPLE CELEBRATED FOR 14 DAYS.

PRAYER PUPS BY JEFFREY SMITH

SOLOMON HAD THE ARK PLACED RIGHT BELOW THE CHERUBIM.

THE CHERU...WHO...WHAT?

CHERUBIM. IT MEANS "ANGELS."

NO JOKIM?

THE ARK OF THE COVENANT CONTAINED THE TEN COMMANDMENTS THAT GOD GAVE TO MOSES.

www.PrayerPups.com

PRAYER PUPS BY JEFFREY SMITH

I'M THINKING THAT IF I DO WHAT GOD SAYS, HE'LL GIVE ME WHAT I REALLY WANT.

YOU SHOULD DO WHAT GOD SAYS AND HOPE YOU GET WHAT HE WANTS YOU TO HAVE.

WHAT IF IT'S NOT WHAT I WANT? IT'LL BE BETTER.

WILL IT BE RED AND LEATHER AND TOTALLY CUTE?

WE SHOULD OBEY GOD IN ALL WE DO WITHOUT EXPECTING ANYTHING IN RETURN.

www.PrayerPups.com

PRAYER PUPS BY JEFFREY SMITH

WHAT DO YOU WANT TO BE WHEN YOU GROW UP?

BIGGER.

BIGGER? THAT'S THE BEST YOU CAN DO?

I FIND THAT SETTING MY SIGHTS LOW HELPS ME SUCCEED MORE OFTEN.

GOD WANTS YOU TO "SHOOT FOR THE STARS," AND HE'LL HELP YOU GET THERE.

www.PrayerPups.com

PRAYER PUPS BY JEFFREY SMITH

IN EPHESIANS, THE WORD PAUL USES TO DESCRIBE GOD'S CREATION OF US IS THE SAME WORD THAT BECAME "POETRY."

SO YOU COULD SAY THAT EACH OF US IS ONE OF GOD'S "POEMS."

NOT ME.

I FEEL MORE LIKE AN UNFINISHED SHORT STORY.

"WE ARE GOD'S WORKMANSHIP, CREATED IN CHRIST JESUS TO DO GOOD WORKS" - EPHESIANS 2:10   www.PrayerPups.com

---

PRAYER PUPS BY JEFFREY SMITH

HOW DID YOUR MATH TEST GO?

NOT WELL. BUT IT'S OKAY.

I TOLD MY TEACHER THAT PAUL SAID GOD "MADE FOOLISH THE WISDOM OF THE WORLD." SO I DON'T NEED TO KNOW MATH.

YOU REALIZE THAT'S NOT WHAT THAT VERSE REALLY MEANS.

TOMORROW, I'M GOING TO TELL MY FOOTBALL COACH WHAT I THINK OF HIM, 'CAUSE GOD "CHOSE THE WEAK THINGS OF THE WORLD TO SHAME THE STRONG."

GOOD LUCK WITH THAT.

READ MORE OF WHAT PAUL WROTE IN HIS LETTER BY CHECKING OUT 1 CORINTHIANS.   www.PrayerPups.com

---

PRAYER PUPS BY JEFFREY SMITH

PROFESSOR AMOS, HOW DO I PROTECT MYSELF FROM EVIL?

PAUL SAYS WE SHOULD WEAR FAITH AND LOVE AS A BREASTPLATE.

AND WE SHOULD USE THE HOPE OF SALVATION AS A HELMET.

CAN I GET THOSE AT A SPORTING GOODS STORE?

YOU CAN READ MORE OF PAUL'S LETTER IN 2 THESSALONIANS.   www.PrayerPups.com

PRAYER PUPS BY JEFFREY SMITH

MANY OF OUR CURRENT LAWS AND CUSTOMS ORIGINALLY CAME FROM THE BIBLE!

www.PrayerPups.com

PRAYER PUPS BY JEFFREY SMITH

IT'S IMPOSSIBLE TO EXPLAIN GOD WITH SCIENCE. IT'S LIKE TRYING TO EXPLAIN MATH WITH A COOKBOOK.

www.PrayerPups.com

PRAYER PUPS BY JEFFREY SMITH

EVEN IF YOU CAN'T CARRY A TUNE, GOD LOVES TO HEAR YOU SING PRAISE TO HIM.

www.PrayerPups.com

PRAYER PUPS BY JEFFREY SMITH

GOD IS IN COMPLETE CONTROL, SO WHEN YOU'RE WORRIED ABOUT SOMETHING, JUST "BE STILL."

www.PrayerPups.com

PRAYER PUPS BY JEFFREY SMITH

MEN LIVED LONGER BEFORE THE FLOOD THAN AFTER IT. ADAM LIVED 920 YEARS, MOSES LIVED ONLY 70.

www.PrayerPups.com

PRAYER PUPS BY JEFFREY SMITH

YOU CAN READ ABOUT JESUS WALKING ON WATER IN MATTHEW 14:22-33, MARK 6:45-52 & JOHN 6:16-21.

www.PrayerPups.com

PRAYER PUPS BY JEFFREY SMITH

"WITH GOD, ALL THINGS ARE POSSIBLE." - MATTHEW 19:26

www.PrayerPups.com

PRAYER PUPS BY JEFFREY SMITH

PRAY FOR YOUR FRIENDS, BUT MAKE SURE YOU HAVE <u>THEIR</u> BEST INTERESTS AT HEART.

www.PrayerPups.com

PRAYER PUPS BY JEFFREY SMITH

ASK GOD RIGHT NOW TO SHOW YOU WHAT YOUR PART IS IN HIS PLAN.

www.PrayerPups.com

PRAYER PUPS BY JEFFREY SMITH

I STARTED OFF THE DAY DOING REALLY WELL IN MY WALK WITH GOD.

I DIDN'T GOSSIP, COMPLAIN, FIB, GET MAD, BE GREEDY, OR DO ANY OF THE THINGS I'VE BEEN TRYING TO CHANGE.

THAT'S GREAT. THEN WHAT HAPPENED?

THE ALARM WENT OFF AND I HAD TO GET OUT OF BED.

SOMETIMES IT'S HARD TO DO WHAT YOU KNOW IS RIGHT, BUT IT'S ALWAYS WORTH TRYING. www.PrayerPups.com

---

PRAYER PUPS BY JEFFREY SMITH

HOW'S IT GOING PRAYING FOR GOD TO CHANGE THE WAY YOU BEHAVE?

ALL RIGHT, I GUESS. WHAT'S WRONG?

THIS MORNING I PRAYED THAT GOD WOULD MAKE ME MORE PATIENT.

SO?

SO? IT'S BEEN FOUR HOURS AND NOTHING!

ALWAYS REMEMBER...GOD IS NOT ON OUR TIMETABLE. WE'RE ON HIS TIMETABLE. www.PrayerPups.com

---

PRAYER PUPS BY JEFFREY SMITH

I'VE BEEN PRAYING FOR GOD TO CHANGE THE WAY I BEHAVE.

LIKE WHAT?

LIKE STAYING FOCUSED ON ONE THING AT A TI... HEY, A SQUIRREL!

I'D KEEP PRAYING IF I WERE YOU.

I LOVE SQUIR... LOOK, A BIRD!

GOD WILL HELP US CHANGE ANYTHING ABOUT OURSELVES THAT WE DON'T LIKE. www.PrayerPups.com

GOD ANSWERS PRAYERS THAT ARE OFFERED UP WITH A SINCERE AND HUMBLE HEART.

YOU CAN LEARN A LOT MORE ABOUT GOD AND ABOUT YOURSELF IF YOU LISTEN TO OTHERS.

GET INVOLVED IN YOUR CHURCH AND YOU'LL SEE THAT YOU CAN DO GREAT THINGS.

PRAYER PUPS BY JEFFREY SMITH

MAKE SURE YOUR QUEST FOR HELP WITH YOUR PROBLEMS DOESN'T MAKE YOU JUDGMENTAL OF OTHERS.   www.PrayerPups.com

PRAYER PUPS BY JEFFREY SMITH

BOTH ADAM AND EVE WENT DEFIED GOD BY EATING FROM THE TREE IN THE MIDDLE OF THE GARDEN OF EDEN.   www.PrayerPups.com

PRAYER PUPS BY JEFFREY SMITH

IT TAKES BRAVERY TO STAND UP TO PEER PRESSURE. PRAY FOR GOD TO GIVE YOU THAT BRAVERY.   www.PrayerPups.com

PRAYER PUPS BY JEFFREY SMITH

LET GOD SPEAK TO YOU AND YOU'LL ALWAYS KNOW RIGHT FROM WRONG.

www.PrayerPups.com

PRAYER PUPS BY JEFFREY SMITH

THE BIBLE IS FULL OF EXCITING STORIES, BUT THERE AREN'T ANY CAR CHASE SCENES!

www.PrayerPups.com

PRAYER PUPS BY JEFFREY SMITH

THE "BEGATS" OF 1 CHRONICLES AND MATTHEW ARE IMPORTANT TO SHOW THE FAMILY LINEAGE OF CHRIST.   www.PrayerPups.com

PRAYER PUPS BY JEFFREY SMITH

HAVE FAITH IN GOD ABOVE ALL ELSE.

www.PrayerPups.com

PRAYER PUPS BY JEFFREY SMITH

IT'S TRUE...THE ONLY DOMESTICATED ANIMAL NEVER MENTIONED IN THE BIBLE IS THE CAT.

www.PrayerPups.com

PRAYER PUPS BY JEFFREY SMITH

WHEN GOD IS ON YOUR SIDE, YOU HAVE NOTHING TO FEAR.

www.PrayerPups.com

PRAYER PUPS BY JEFFREY SMITH

THE TEST TO GET INTO HEAVEN IS ONLY ONE SENTENCE: DO YOU ACCEPT JESUS CHRIST AS YOUR SAVIOR?   www.PrayerPups.com

PRAYER PUPS BY JEFFREY SMITH

CALMING THE SEAS IS ONE OF THE STORIES THAT PROVES JESUS WAS THE SON OF GOD.   www.PrayerPups.com

PRAYER PUPS BY JEFFREY SMITH

GOD WORKED THROUGH MOSES TO ACCOMPLISH MANY MIRACLES.   www.PrayerPups.com

PRAYER PUPS BY JEFFREY SMITH

BOTH MATTHEW 4 AND LUKE 4 TELL OF SATAN TEMPTING JESUS TO SHOW HIS POWER.

www.PrayerPups.com

PRAYER PUPS BY JEFFREY SMITH

LUKE 4:16 SAYS THAT ON THE SABBATH, JESUS "WENT INTO THE SYNAGOGUE, AS WAS HIS CUSTOM."

www.PrayerPups.com

PRAYER PUPS BY JEFFREY SMITH

FINDING OUT SOMEONE DOESN'T BELIEVE IN GOD SHOULD BE YOUR CUE TO TELL THEM ABOUT JESUS!

www.PrayerPups.com

PRAYER PUPS BY JEFFREY SMITH

SOME PEOPLE WILL MAKE FUN OF YOUR FAITH. MAKE SURE TO PRAY FOR THEM TO COME TO JESUS.   www.PrayerPups.com

PRAYER PUPS BY JEFFREY SMITH

IT'S OFTEN EASY TO CHALLENGE A NON-BELIEVER'S REASONS FOR DOUBTING GOD.   www.PrayerPups.com

PRAYER PUPS BY JEFFREY SMITH

GIVING THANKS ISN'T ONLY FOR THANKSGIVING...KEEP THAT GRATITUDE IN YOUR HEART ALL YEAR LONG!   www.PrayerPups.com

PRAYER PUPS BY JEFFREY SMITH

I'M NOT SAYING CHRISTIANS AREN'T SMART, JUST UNABLE TO SEE THINGS FROM A NEW PERSPECTIVE.

YOU MEAN LIKE SIR ISAAC NEWTON, WHO ACTUALLY WROTE MORE ABOUT GOD THAN HE DID ABOUT MATH? OR COPERNICUS OR KEPLER OR DESCARTES OR GALILEO, WHO WROTE "GOD IS KNOWN BY NATURE IN HIS WORKS AND BY DOCTRINE IN HIS REVEALED WORD"?

SO'S YOUR OLD MAN!

GOOD COMEBACK.

DON'T <u>EVER</u> LET ANYONE QUESTION YOUR INTELLIGENCE SIMPLY BECAUSE YOU'RE A CHRISTIAN.   www.PrayerPups.com

---

PRAYER PUPS BY JEFFREY SMITH

LOOK, DT, BEFORE YOU LEAVE, I HAVE TO TELL YOU SOMETHING.

SHOOT.

PLEASE GIVE JESUS A CHANCE IN YOUR LIFE. I WROTE DOWN A FEW BOOKS YOU MIGHT WANT TO CHECK OUT.

BOOK

WELL...NO PROMISES, CON. BUT I WON'T SAY NO.

THAT'S A START. THANK YOU, GOD!

YOU WON'T OFTEN BRING SOMEONE TO CHRIST. USUALLY, YOU'LL JUST PLANT A SEED THAT GOD WILL GROW.   www.PrayerPups.com

---

PRAYER PUPS BY JEFFREY SMITH

DEAR DIARY-TO-GOD...

I'VE BEEN READING THE OLD TESTAMENT. 2 SAMUEL, IN PARTICULAR.

IN THE STORY WHERE DAVID IS MERCIFUL TO MEPHIBOSHETH, I JUST HAVE ONE QUESTION...

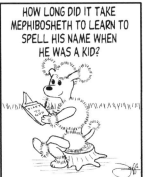

HOW LONG DID IT TAKE MEPHIBOSHETH TO LEARN TO SPELL HIS NAME WHEN HE WAS A KID?

MEPHIBOSHETH WAS CRIPPLED AND KING DAVID HAD HIM EAT AT HIS TABLE FOR THE REST OF HIS LIFE.   www.PrayerPups.com

PRAYER PUPS BY JEFFREY SMITH

WOULDN'T IT BE GREAT IF WE ALL WERE SO FILLED WITH THE SPIRIT THAT WE CHEERED FOR JESUS?   www.PrayerPups.com

PRAYER PUPS BY JEFFREY SMITH

JOHN THE BAPTIST WAS JUST ONE OF MANY PEOPLE IN THE BIBLE WHO PROPHESIED THE COMING CHRIST.   www.PrayerPups.com

PRAYER PUPS BY JEFFREY SMITH

ISAIAH 11 SPEAKS PROPHECY ABOUT THE COMING OF JESUS CHRIST.   www.PrayerPups.com

PRAYER PUPS BY JEFFREY SMITH

ALWAYS DO WHAT IS RIGHT, EVEN WHEN NO ONE KNOWS YOU DID IT...BECAUSE GOD KNOWS!   www.PrayerPups.com

PRAYER PUPS BY JEFFREY SMITH

JUST BECAUSE GOD KNOWS EVERYTHING ABOUT YOU DOESN'T MEAN HE DOESN'T WANT TO TALK WITH YOU.   www.PrayerPups.com

PRAYER PUPS BY JEFFREY SMITH

THE TRIANGLE SHAPE OF A CHRISTMAS TREE SHOULD REMIND YOU OF THE HOLY TRINITY.   www.PrayerPups.com

PRAYER PUPS BY JEFFREY SMITH

NIM, I'M SO GLAD YOU HAVE SOME CANNED GOODS FOR THE CHURCH FOOD DRIVE!

YEP!

AND NOT A PLENTY IN THE BUNCH.

NOT A WHAT IN THE BUNCH?

A PLENTY. I SEPARATED THE "GOODS" FROM THE "PLENTIES" BEFORE I FILLED THE CAN.

AND VOILA! CANNED "GOODS"!

PATIENCE... HE MEANS WELL.

REMEMBER TO HELP THOSE LESS FORTUNATE THIS CHRISTMAS SEASON.

PRAYER PUPS BY JEFFREY SMITH

OKAY, I UNDERSTAND THE GOLD.

MMM, HMM.

AND I GET THE MYRRH.

HERE IT COMES.

BY WHY FRANKENSTEIN? WOULDN'T HE JUST SCARE BABY JESUS?

NOT "FRANKENSTEIN." FRANKINCENSE. IT'S AN AROMATIC RESIN USED IN CREATING PERFUME.

OH! WELL, THAT'S A MUCH BETTER GIFT THAN A MONSTER.

YA THINK?

THE GIFTS THE THREE WISE MEN GAVE BABY JESUS WERE VERY TREASURED DURING THAT TIME.

PRAYER PUPS BY JEFFREY SMITH

CAN YOU EVEN IMAGINE HOW AWESOME IT WAS 2000 YEARS AGO TO LEARN THAT JESUS WAS ACTUALLY BORN?

ALL OF MANKIND HAD WAITED ON MESSIAH FOR CENTURIES AND SUDDENLY...HE WAS WITH US. THAT'S WHAT HIS NAME MEANS..."GOD WITH US."

THE AIR MUST HAVE SMELLED SWEETER. THE SUN'S LIGHT MUST HAVE BEEN BRIGHTER. EVERY LIVING CREATURE ON EARTH MUST HAVE FELT AN URGE TO BEND ITS KNEE AND BOW ITS HEAD.

THAT WAS BEAUTIFUL. BUT I JUST HAVE ONE QUESTION: WHO ARE YOU AND WHAT HAVE YOU DONE WITH NIM?

GOD "BEING WITH US" WAS SO HARD TO IMAGINE THAT EVEN JOHN THE BAPTIST NEEDED CONFIRMATION.

PRAYER PUPS BY JEFFREY SMITH

ALL THROUGH THE MONTH OF DECEMBER, THINK ABOUT THE MIRACLE OF JESUS' BIRTH.

PRAYER PUPS BY JEFFREY SMITH

IT'S ONLY 15 DAYS UNTIL CHRISTMAS! THIS WOULD BE A GOOD TIME TO READ MATTHEW 1:18-25.

PRAYER PUPS BY JEFFREY SMITH

YOU ARE IMPORTANT TO GOD. JOHN 15:16 SAYS "YOU HAVE NOT CHOSEN ME, BUT I HAVE CHOSEN YOU."

PRAYER PUPS BY JEFFREY SMITH

BOTH JOSEPHS WERE IMPORTANT, BUT AT CHRISTMAS TIME, IT'S GOOD TO LEARN ABOUT MARY'S HUSBAND.   www.PrayerPups.com

PRAYER PUPS BY JEFFREY SMITH

JOSEPH HAD TO TRAVEL TO BETHLEHEM FOR THE CENSUS BECAUSE IT WAS THE TOWN OF HIS BIRTH.   www.PrayerPups.com

PRAYER PUPS BY JEFFREY SMITH

THERE ARE MANY STRONG WOMEN IN THE BIBLE. ASK YOUR PASTOR WHERE TO FIND THEM.   www.PrayerPups.com

PRAYER PUPS BY JEFFREY SMITH

WHEN YOU LET JESUS INTO YOUR HEART, YOUR SOUL WILL BE SAVED.

PRAYER PUPS BY JEFFREY SMITH

ADVENT IS TIME OF ANTICIPATION, HOPE AND NEW BEGINNINGS.

PRAYER PUPS BY JEFFREY SMITH

MAKE SURE TO TAKE TIME TO SING CHRISTMAS CAROLS THIS SEASON...NO MATTER WHAT YOU SOUND LIKE!

ACKNOWLEDGEMENTS

There are so many people to thank and I know I'll leave someone out, so please understand that this isn't a comprehensive list. If it appears I've overlooked someone, it's entirely my fault and I apologize for the oversight.

Matt, Amy, Zane, Sarah and Bekah Miller for your encouragement and help during the difficult times. You are truly great friends.

My mother, Sandy Johnson for supporting me as I developed my creative side and for always being there.

My stepfather, Jerry Johnson for his advice as I struggled to bring the Prayer Pups to life.

Dr. Kevin McCallon, Maury Gill, Sharon Wood, Jonathan Brown and all the good folks at Kingwood First Baptist Church for your help and support as I was creating the initial Prayer Pups comics.

Dr. Mike Barnett of Ocean Springs Baptist Church for being the first customer for The Good Newz Children's Church Bulletins featuring the Prayer Pups.

All the churches and other groups that have used the Prayer Pups in their ministries around the world.

And most of all, my beautiful wife, Sebrina Zerkus Smith, who has supported me through all of my crazy hare-brained schemes, including the idea of being a Christian Cartoonist. Here's to another wonderful 25 years!

Do Your Kids Know The Good Newz?

Put The Prayer Pups To Work For Your Church Today!

- Children's bulletins for 3 distinct age groups
- Comic strips featuring the Prayer Pups
- Puzzles & word searches
- Weekly devotionals
- Jokes and riddles
- Coloring pages
- And much more
- Less than $50!

A full year on
one convenient CD!

www.TheGoodNewz.com

Made in the USA
San Bernardino, CA
20 March 2017